Healthiest Vegetables

Healthiest Vegetables

Emily Ezekiel
Photography by Issy Croker

Contents

Introduction

Vegetables are an essential part of our diet. Their history reaches into the distant years of hunters and gatherers, and today throughout the world we have a huge range of vegetable varieties readily available to grow ourselves or to buy. We need to eat vegetables every day simply because there are no other food groups that can provide the body with all the nutrients it needs to be healthy and functioning at its best. Not only do vegetables provide all the essential vitamins and minerals needed for daily health, but they have been shown to reduce the risk of and protect against a number of chronic diseases.

WHAT IS SO GOOD ABOUT VEGETABLES?

- Vegetables are the richest source of dietary fiber for the body. Food cannot move effectively through our digestive system without fiber.
- Vegetables are an important source of many vitamins and minerals, including vitamins A, B, C, K, folate, potassium, magnesium, calcium.
- Vegetables are a source of antioxidants and phytonutrients. Phytonutrients, such as carotenoids and flavonoids, give vegetables their rich colors and diverse flavors and can simply not be found in any other food group.
- Vegetables do not have cholesterol and are mostly naturally low in fat.

Although some vitamins can be stored within the body for later use, many can't, so we need to make sure we are constantly replenishing and providing what our bodies need. We can easily go a whole day without eating any fresh produce, so looking over the essential vitamins & minerals chart (opposite) is a great way to reflect on what we need and how we can increase the amounts we are getting by increasing the number of vegetables we eat.

essential vitamins & minerals

VITAMIN		VEGETABLES THAT CONTAIN IT
Vitamin A	→	Carotenoids in carrots, bell peppers, tomatoes, spinach, watercress
Vitamin B6	→	beets, sweet potatoes, bell peppers, onions, garlic
Vitamin C	→	broccoli, bell peppers, sweet potatoes, tomatoes, cauliflower, garlic
Vitamin K	→	spinach, watercress, cauliflower
Calcium	→	kale, beets, sweet potatoes
Iron	→	spinach, watercress, broccoli, cauliflower, kale
Magnesium	→	spinach, broccoli, peas, sprouts, cauliflower
Folate	→	spinach, broccoli, bell peppers, beets
Potassium	→	carrots, bell peppers, beets, cauliflower, tomatoes, sweet potatoes
Zinc	→	sprouts, peas

Eat the rainbow

Ideally when consuming vegetables, it is good to eat a range of colors and different types of vegetables to fulfill the needs of our bodies. Botanically, vegetables are divided into a number of plant families. Often vegetables in the same plant family contain similar vitamins, minerals, and antioxidants. The vegetables in this book come from a number of different vegetable families, and combining them into your diet will give you all the nutrients you need.

It is a great idea to mix up the way you consume your vegetables. The recipes in this book will show you that you don't have to miss out on delicious dishes to make sure you include vegetables in each meal. Juice them raw for one meal, have a salad or cook a couple of different types of vegetables for another. Be aware of the quantity of fresh vegetables you eat and try to increase the amount and variety.

WHAT CAN THESE VEGETABLES DO FOR ME?
Your body will benefit in many ways from increasing your intake of these vegetables. Some people will benefit more than others, depending on their bodies current health.

- Vegetables contain a high amount of dietary fiber, which maintains a good digestive system.
- Risk of heart disease, diabetes, and obesity is reduced when you eat vegetables.
- The antioxidants contained in vegetables can protect and reduce the risk of cancers.
- Eating vegetables will reduce cholesterol levels and calorie intake.
- Vitamin-rich foods increase immune system strength and help to ward off sickness.
- Minerals contained in vitamins increase the body's ability to absorb vitamins.

spinach & watercress

Spinach is from the amaranth family and is used in many cultures around the world. The dark leafy green is an excellent source of iron. Watercress is from the brassica family and is mainly used as a garnish, but has recently become more popular in cooking.

what's in them?

Spinach: 1 cup (30 g) raw spinach is mostly made up of water. It contains:

- Full daily requirement of vitamin K
- 30 mg calcium
- 0.81 g iron
- Vitamins C and A
- Magnesium
- Folate
- Thiamine, fiber, phosphorus, alpha-lipoic acid

Watercress: 1 cup (35 g) watercress contains:

- 0.8 g protein
- Full daily requirement of vitamin K
- 50% daily requirement of vitamins C and A
- Calcium
- Manganese
- Potassium
- Vitamin E, thiamine, riboflavin, magnesium, and phosphorus
- Folate
- Fiber, alpha- lipoic acid

what can they do for me?

As well as being a great source of iron and calcium, the antioxidants in spinach may help lower blood pressure and keep the heart healthy. The high levels of vitamin K in both spinach and watercress are good for bones and improve calcium absorption.

how to eat these greens

Both spinach and watercress can be eaten raw and cooked. Use the leaves raw to make salads and smoothies or cook in a soup or side dish, or add them to pastas, stews, and pies.

varieties

Both of these greens are readily available in a number of varieties, including as microgreens. Baby spinach leaves are much softer and more commonly used fresh for salads, etc. Here are some of the well-known varieties:

spinach

SAVOY

BABY SPINACH

watercress

WATERCRESS can be harvested wild and has also been cultivated for commercial growth, with some land cress variations too. It is also available as sprouts.

other varieties

There are many close relations to spinach that are often labeled as spinach:

- **CHARD:** Plain green leaves with white or multicolored stems
- **FLAT-LEAF SPINACH:** Smooth spade-shaped leaves with a slightly sweet flavor
- **ATRIPLEX SPINACH:** Also called orach, this is grown as an alternative to spinach
- **GOOD KING HENRY SPINACH:** Also called poor man's spinach, this perennial plant is cooked and eaten just like spinach
- **LAND CRESS:** Also called American cress, this looks and tastes like watercress

how to cook spinach

type of veg	quantity for 2	quantity for 4	cooking vessel	quantity of liquid	salt	oil / butter

steam

type of veg	quantity for 2	quantity for 4	cooking vessel	quantity of liquid	salt	oil / butter
Spinach	6½ cups (200 g)		↑ steamer ↓	↑ ¾ inch (2 cm) water in steamer ↓	↑ 1 teaspoon ↓	↑ 1 tablespoon either ↓
Watercress	5¾ cups (200 g)					

bake

type of veg	quantity for 2	quantity for 4	cooking vessel	quantity of liquid	salt	oil / butter
Spinach	↑ 1 lb. (450 g) ↓		↑ medium baking sheet ↓		↑ 1 teaspoon ↓	↑ 1 tablespoon either ↓

fry

type of veg	quantity for 2	quantity for 4	cooking vessel	quantity of liquid	salt	oil / butter
Spinach	11 cups (350 g)		↑ large nonstick skillet ↓	↑	↑ 1 teaspoon ↓	1 tablespoon peanut oil
Watercress	5¾ cups (200 g)					1 tablespoon butter

soup

type of veg	quantity for 2	quantity for 4	cooking vessel	quantity of liquid	salt	oil / butter
Spinach	↑ yes ↓	↑ 1 lb. (450 g) ↓	↑ large nonstick saucepan ↓	4¼ cups (1 L) broth	↑ 1 teaspoon ↓	2 tablespoons olive oil
Watercress				5 cups (1.2 L) broth		2 tablespoons butter

and watercress

other ingredients	heat	with lid	cooking time	notes
↑ 3 garlic cloves, chopped; 1 chili pepper, diced; and juice of ½ lemon ↓	↑ medium ↓	↑ yes ↓	3 min. 5 min.	Perfect served as a side alongside fresh fish, broiled meats, and baked veg for a healthy meal. An easy way of eating greens. Best steamed, then stir through broccoli or cauli-rice. Or simply steam and add to soups.
14 oz. (400 g) can tomatoes or 1 cup (200 g) crème fraîche or sour cream, and juice of 1 lemon	↑ 350°F (180°C) ↓	↑ cover with foil ↓	↑ 5–8 min. ↓	Baked spinach can be really versatile. Use it as a base for breakfast eggs or stir in crème fraîche and toss in spaghetti for a simple pasta.
diced ginger, garlic, and soy sauce ½ bunch of sage, juice and zest of ½ lemon	medium-high high	↑ no ↓	↑ 3 min. ↓	Heat a large pan, then add oil, garlic, ginger, and fry for a few minutes. Add soy sauce and spinach and cook until wilted. Heat a large pan, then add butter and sage and fry for a few minutes. Add lemon juice and zest and watercress and cook until wilted.
1 leek, chopped; 1 Maris Piper potato, peeled and diced; 2 celery sticks, chopped; 3 garlic cloves, diced 1 onion, diced; 1 sweet potato, peeled and diced; 1 red chili pepper; generous 1 cup (200 ml) crème fraîche or sour cream	↑ medium ↓	↑ yes ↓	10–15 min. 15–20 min.	Heat oil, add chopped vegetables, and fry until slightly soft. Pour in broth, bring to a boil, and cook for 5–10 min. Add spinach and cook for 5 min. Leave chunky or blend until smooth. Heat butter, onions and sweet potato in a pan for 10 min. Add broth and chili pepper and bring to a boil. Cover and cook until sweet potato is tender. Add watercress and creme fraîche or sour cream and serve.

15 min. / 20 min.

These fluffy, light, and zesty muffins are great for picnics, light lunches, and snacks. They are full of vitamin C. Serve with a zesty green salad.

Spinach & ricotta muffins

Makes: 9 large muffins

6½ cups (200 g) baby spinach, roughly chopped

1 red chili pepper, seeded and chopped

finely grated zest of 1 lemon

1 cup (250 ml) milk

5 tablespoons (70 ml) olive oil

3 large eggs

3⅓ cups (400 g) spelt flour

2 teaspoons baking powder

salt and pepper

½ cup (125 g) ricotta

Preheat the oven to 350°F (180°C). Line two jumbo muffin pans with 9 paper liners.

Place the spinach in a large bowl with the chopped chili pepper and lemon zest.

In another bowl, whisk together the milk and olive oil, then whisk in the eggs, one at a time. Fold in the flour and baking powder and season well with salt and pepper. Tip in the spinach mixture and mix well. Gently fold in the ricotta, leaving it semi-unmixed. Pour the batter into the muffin liners until they are a third full and bake for 20 minutes, or until golden and cooked through.

Carefully remove the pan from the oven and let rest in the pan for 2 minutes. Transfer to a wire rack to cool slightly before serving warm or cold.

15 min. / 25 min.

Spinach, watercress, & feta filo tart

Serves: 6 for lunch and 4 for dinner

⅓ cup (50 g) pine nuts
5 large eggs
7 oz. (200 g) feta, crumbled
pepper
1 tablespoon dried oregano
finely grated zest and juice of 1 lemon
½ cup (113 g) unsalted butter, at room temperature, plus extra for greasing
½ cup (115 ml) olive oil
6½ cups (200 g) baby spinach
8½ cups (300 g) watercress
9½ oz. (270 g) pack filo pastry

Preheat the oven to 400°F (200°C).

Toast the pine nuts in a large dry skillet over medium heat for 1 minute, or until golden, tossing so they don't burn. Set aside.

Break the eggs into a bowl and add the feta. Season with pepper, add the oregano, lemon zest, and toasted pine nuts and mix well.

Melt half the butter and the oil in the skillet over medium heat. Add half the spinach and stir until wilted, then add the remaining spinach. Do the same with the watercress, stirring until wilted. Remove from the heat and add the lemon juice.

Grease a 9½-inch (24 cm) oven-safe skillet with butter. Lay a filo sheet over the base, then brush with butter. Continue with the remaining filo and butter, moving the sheets clockwise around the pan.

Stir the wilted greens into the egg mixture, then pour the filling into the pastry case and spread out evenly. Fold the filo up and over the filling to cover. Place the pan over medium heat for 5 minutes, then bake on the top shelf of the oven for 20 minutes, or until golden and crisp.

15 min. / 30 min.

This makes the most perfect creamy and light side curry or main dish. Serve alongside broiled meat and fresh roti and rice for an authentic feast.

Indian spinach & paneer curry

Serves: 4 as a side

4 tablespoons ghee
2 large white onions,
finely sliced
1 teaspoon ground
turmeric
2 teaspoons Kashmiri
chili powder
grated zest and juice
of 1 lemon, plus extra
juice if needed
1 lb. (450 g) paneer,
cut into 1¼-inch (3 cm)
cubes
1 lb (500 g) fresh
spinach
6 garlic cloves, grated
2½–3½-inch (6–9 cm)
piece of ginger, peeled
and grated
1 green chili pepper,
roughly chopped
salt

Heat 2 tablespoons of the ghee in a large skillet over medium heat. Add the onions and fry for 10–15 minutes until soft.

Meanwhile, mix the turmeric, chili powder, and lemon juice and zest together in a bowl. Add the paneer and toss well. Set aside.

Place the spinach in a colander, pour over boiling water, and drain. Transfer the spinach to a dish towel and squeeze out excess water.

Scoop the onions out of the pan and set aside. Add the remaining ghee to the pan, then add the paneer and fry over medium heat for about 8 minutes, tossing the pan so the paneer becomes golden all over. Scoop out the paneer and set aside on a plate, leaving the spices behind in the pan. Add the garlic, ginger, and chopped chili pepper to the pan and lightly fry for 4 minutes, stirring constantly. Add the onions back to the pan with ½ cup (115 ml) water, then add the spinach and paneer and cook for 3 minutes, stirring constantly. Season with salt and a little extra lemon juice if needed.

TIP

If you are planning on taking this soup out for lunch, keep the garlic crisps and croutons in a separate container so they stay crunchy.

vegetarian / nut-free

Watercress soup with crispy garlic & croutons

Serves: 4–6

½ cup (115 ml) olive oil
6 garlic cloves, finely sliced
5 tablespoons (70 g) butter
2 celery sticks, chopped
2 onions, chopped
14 oz. (400 g) can chickpeas, drained and rinsed
6⅓ cups (1.5 L) vegetable broth
11½ cups (400 g) watercress
salt and pepper

Croutons

5 oz. (150 g) sourdough bread, torn into large chunks
3 tablespoons (45 ml) olive oil
grated zest and juice of 1 lemon

Preheat the oven to 350°F (180°C).

Heat the olive oil in a pan over medium heat, add the garlic and stir-fry for 3 minutes until colored and crispy. Remove with a slotted spoon and set aside. Pour out half the garlic oil and reserve for serving.

Add the butter to the garlic oil left in the pan, then add the celery, onions, and a large pinch of salt and cook for 15 minutes, or until soft and translucent. Add the chickpeas with the broth and bring to a gentle simmer. Cook for 15–20 minutes.

Meanwhile, make the croutons. Mix the torn bread, olive oil, and lemon zest together on a baking sheet. Bake for 10 minutes, tossing halfway through, until golden and crisp. Set aside.

Remove 2 ladles of chickpeas from the broth and purée the soup with a handheld blender. Add the watercress, leave to wilt, then blend until the watercress is finely chopped. Return the reserved chickpeas to the soup and add the lemon juice. Season. Serve the soup topped with the croutons, garlic, and a drizzle of the remaining garlic oil.

Watercress contains lots of vitamin K. Serve this salad with crusty bread on even the coldest days.

Watercress, pea, & burrata salad with a zesty dressing

Serves: 4

1⅓ cups (200 g) peas

2 mint sprigs

2 scallions, finely sliced

2 balls burrata

5¾ cups (200 g) watercress

1 small bunch of mint, leaves picked, and large ones torn

Dressing

4 tablespoons (60 ml) olive oil

grated zest and juice of 1 lemon

1 tablespoon Dijon mustard

salt and pepper

1 red chili pepper, seeded and finely chopped

Bring a large pan of salted water to a boil and add the peas and mint sprigs. Cook for 1 minute, then plunge into ice-cold water.

Drain the peas and place on a serving platter along with the scallions, balls of burrata, and watercress.

To make the dressing, whisk together the olive oil, lemon zest and juice, mustard, and a good pinch of salt and pepper until well emulsified and thickened. Stir through the chili pepper, then spoon over the salad and sprinkle over the mint leaves. Serve immediately.

TIP

vegetarian / nut-free

You can build the salad up with any leftover veg and beans and lentils. If you need extra carbs, simply add some chopped boiled potatoes or torn naan bread.

Indian spinach salad with spicy yogurt dressing

Serves: 4

1 red onion, finely diced

4 mixed carrots, peeled into long strips

10 cups (300 g) spinach

14 oz. (400 g) can chickpeas, drained and rinsed

seeds from
1 pomegranate

1 bunch of cilantro leaves, chopped

4 papadums, lightly crushed

Dressing

1 teaspoon garam masala

1 green chili pepper, finely chopped

1 cup (225 g) plain yogurt

2 tablespoons tamarind chutney

Mix all the salad ingredients together in a large bowl and set aside.

Mix the dressing ingredients, except the chutney, together in a small bowl.

Plate up the salad and drizzle over the dressing, finishing with equal drizzles of tamarind chutney. Serve immediately.

This pilaf is simple and really quick, especially if you use leftover chicken. If you don't have any, simply roast 4–5 skinless, boneless chicken thighs at 350°F (180°C) for 25 minutes, or until golden and cooked, then shred it.

Speedy chicken & spinach pilaf

Serves: 4
2 tablespoons ghee
2 onions, finely sliced
2 tablespoons garam masala
1 teaspoon chili pepper flakes
1 teaspoon ground turmeric
¾ lb. (300 g) roasted chicken, shredded
2¾ cups (500 g) cooked basmati rice
10 cups (300 g) baby spinach, chopped
juice of 1 lemon
salt and pepper

To serve
6 tablespoons (85 grams) plain yogurt
1 bunch of cilantro, leaves picked

Heat the ghee in a large skillet, add the onions, and fry for 10–15 minutes until softened and starting to turn golden. Add the spices and fry for 2 minutes. Add the chicken and cooked rice and stir for 5 minutes, or until heated through. You may need to add a splash of water if it is sticking to the base of the pan. Stir in the spinach and lemon juice and season well with salt and pepper. Cover with a lid and cook for another 4 minutes, or until wilted.

Serve the pilaf topped with dollops of yogurt and cilantro.

kale

Kale is a part of the brassica or cruciferous family and is a cultivar of cabbage grown for its edible leaves.

what's in it?

Kale is very low in calories. It is made up of 84% water, 9% carbs, 4% protein, and 1% fat. 1 cup (65 g) kale is

- 7 calories
- A rich source of vitamins A, C, and K
- High in minerals iron, calcium, potassium, and phosphorus
- Rich in phytochemicals including sulforaphane and ferulic acid

what can it do for me?

Kale is shown to benefit people with high cholesterol. In a study undertaken over 12 weeks, men who drank a kale juice daily showed a 10% reduction in bad cholesterol and a 27% increase in good cholesterol. Kale is also shown to reduce blood pressure, blood cholesterol, and stabilize blood sugar levels.

how to eat kale

Kale can be used in many dishes, including in pasta, salads, and sandwiches. It can be baked into chips, juiced, and finely chopped to be consumed raw as well as steamed, sautéed, and boiled. Kale can be tough to chew if eaten raw, but can be softened by massaging with oil and removing the central stem.

varieties

There are many different types of kale. The flavors and texture of leaf differ between them all. The cultivars are differentiated by the leaf type:

GREEN CURLY KALE (Scots kale)

KAI LAN (a Chinese cultivar)

PURPLE KALE

ORNAMENTAL KALE
in a variety of colors (still edible but not as palatable)

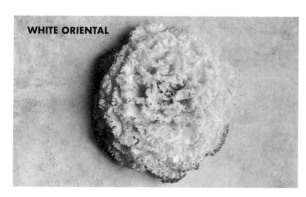

WHITE ORIENTAL

other varieties

There are numerous other varieties of kale, such as:

- **RED URSA**: Beautiful deep-red leaves, this kale has a tender flavor

- **RUSSIAN KALE** (plain leaf): This is the sweetest of all kale and works well in risottos

- **CAVOLO NERO** (bumpy dark flat leaf): Also called Tuscan kale, the leaves are very dark green, almost black

- **BABY KALE**: This is the term for the tender young kale leaves

- **JERSEY KALE**: This kale can grow to 5 feet (1.5 m) in height; the large leaves can be cooked like cabbage

how to cook kale

type of veg	quantity for 2	quantity for 4	cooking vessel	quantity of liquid	salt	oil / butter

steam

type of veg	quantity for 2	quantity for 4	cooking vessel	quantity of liquid	salt	oil / butter
Kale	2¼ cups (150 g)		steamer	¾ inch (2 cm) water in steamer	1½ teaspoons	1 teaspoon either

bake/roast

type of veg	quantity for 2	quantity for 4	cooking vessel	quantity of liquid	salt	oil / butter
Kale	3 cups (200 g)		large flat baking sheet		1½ teaspoons	1 tablespoon oil

fry

type of veg	quantity for 2	quantity for 4	cooking vessel	quantity of liquid	salt	oil / butter
Kale	3 cups (200 g)		large nonstick skillet		½ teaspoon	1 tablespoon either

soup

type of veg	quantity for 2	quantity for 4	cooking vessel	quantity of liquid	salt	oil / butter
Kale		4½ cups (300 g)	large stockpot	5 cups (1.2 L) vegetable broth	to taste	1 tablespoon olive oil

other ingredients	heat	with lid	cooking time	notes
juice and zest of ½ lemon; 2 garlic cloves, sliced and sautéed; chili pepper flakes	↑ medium ↓	↑ yes ↓	↑ 7 min. ↓	Discard tough ribs of the kale and tear into large pieces. Don't overfill the steamer. Steam for about 7 minutes, or until tender. If undercooked it can be chewy and unpleasant.
↑ pinch of Chinese five-spice powder ↓	↑ 400°F (200°C) ↓	↑ no ↓	↑ 15 min. ↓	For quick, crispy kale, massage oil, salt and pepper, and a pinch of five-spice into the kale and spread in an even thin layer on a large baking sheet. Roast for 15 minutes, turning halfway to ensure you get an even crispness.
↑ 3 garlic cloves, thinly sliced; freshly grated nutmeg ↓	↑ medium-high ↓	↑ no ↓	↑ 5-6 min. ↓	Heat the oil in the pan, add the garlic and cook until golden, then remove from the pan and set aside. Add the kale to the pan and season well. Cook until the kale has softened and started to catch some color. Serve with the garlic and nutmeg.
↑ 1 onion, 1 leek, 1 fennel bulb, 2 garlic cloves, all chopped ↓	↑ medium ↓	↑ no ↓	↑ 40 min. ↓	Heat the oil in the pan and gently sauté the onion, leek, and fennel until soft. Add the garlic and cook for 1 minute. Add the roughly chopped kale, cover with broth, and simmer for 30 minutes. Blend the soup with a stick blender until smooth. Season to taste and serve.

10 min. / 20 min.

These healthy, crunchy spiced kale chips can be stored in an airtight container for up to 3 days if you can keep them that long.

Kale chips with a spicy salt

**Serves: 4 as
a light snack**

½ teaspoon dried chili pepper flakes

½ teaspoon ground turmeric

½ teaspoon cracked black pepper

½ teaspoon sea salt

3 cups (200 g) curly kale leaves, washed and dried

2 tablespoons canola oil

Preheat the oven to 250°F (120°C). Line 2 large baking sheets with parchment paper.

Mix the spices, pepper, and salt together in a small bowl.

Place the kale in a large bowl and drizzle in the oil. Scrunch all the leaves together, giving it all a good massage. Add the seasoning and toss until the kale is evenly coated all over.

Spread the leaves out in a single layer on the prepared baking sheets and bake for about 20 minutes, or until the leaves are crisp, turning the trays halfway through baking so the heat is evenly distributed. Serve immediately.

PREP / COOK TIME

10 min. / 0 min.

TIP

vegetarian / gluten-free

If you would like to make this salad vegan,
then use maple syrup instead of the honey.

Raw kale salad
with tahini & dates

Serves: 2

2¼ cups (150 g) mixed
curly kale, thick stems
removed

juice of 1 lime

1 tablespoon tahini

1 teaspoon honey

1 teaspoon sriracha
chili sauce

¼ teaspoon toasted
sesame oil

1 tablespoon olive oil

⅓ cup (50 g) toasted
hazelnuts

4 Medjool dates,
pitted and sliced

salt and pepper

Lay the kale in a flat pile, roll up tightly lengthwise, and slice
into thin strips. Place in a large bowl and add half the lime juice.
Season with salt and mix really well with your hands, massaging
the juice into the kale. Set aside.

Whisk the tahini, honey, remaining lime juice, sriracha, sesame oil,
and olive oil until smooth. The dressing at this point will be thick,
so gradually add a little cold water until it is creamy, but not
too runny.

Add the hazelnuts, dates, and half the dressing to the kale and mix
well. Season with salt and pepper and serve with the rest of the
dressing on the side.

PREP / COOK TIME

10 min. / 20 min.

TIP

vegetarian / gluten-free

This is a warming green breakfast/brunch, all done in one pan and with minimal prep. Serve with warm flatbreads and steaming coffee to start the day.

One-pan kale with baked eggs

Serves: 2

4 tablespoons (60 ml) olive oil

3 garlic cloves, sliced

4 shallots, finely sliced

10 large tomatoes, roughly chopped

3 cups (200 g) finely chopped kale

3¼ cups (100 g) baby spinach

4 large eggs

salt and pepper

3 tablespoons dukkah

chopped red chili pepper, to garnish (optional)

Preheat the oven to 400°F (200°C). Place a rack on the middle shelf of the oven.

Heat the olive oil, garlic, and shallots in a 9-inch (23 cm) oven-safe skillet and fry over high heat for 5 minutes, or until they have softened a little. Add the tomatoes and fry for another 5 minutes, or until they have started to dry a little.

Add the kale and spinach and fry until the spinach has wilted. Remove from the heat. Using the back of a spoon, make 4 wells for the eggs to sit in. Break the eggs into the wells and season. Bake in the oven for 5–8 minutes until the egg whites are set and the yolk are runny. Sprinkle with the dukkah and a little chopped red chili pepper, if you like.

PREP / COOK TIME

10 min. / 35 min.

TIP

You can make extra salad and have it for lunch
the next day without the egg if you like.

vegetarian / gluten-free

Warm winter kale salad with poached egg & toasted hazelnuts

Serves: 4

½ acorn squash, about
1½ lb. (700 g), seeded
6 tablespoons (90 ml)
extra virgin olive oil
2 tablespoons red wine
vinegar
3 cups (200 g) purple
kale, leaves torn from
stems into bite-sized
pieces
2¾ cups (250 g) purple
sprouting broccoli
juice from 1 orange
1 teaspoon runny honey
4 large eggs
3 tablespoons (30 g)
blanched hazelnuts,
toasted and chopped
1 large bunch of chervil,
leaves picked
salt and pepper

Preheat the oven to 400°F (200°C).

Slice the squash about ¾ inch (2 cm) thick, and place on a large baking sheet. Drizzle with 3 tablespoons of the olive oil and 1 tablespoon of the vinegar, then season. Roast for 30 minutes, tossing halfway through. After 20 minutes, add the kale and roast for 10 minutes.

Place a large griddle pan over high heat. Drizzle 1 tablespoon of the olive oil over the broccoli, then lay on the griddle pan and cook until charred all over. Set aside.

For the dressing, mix the orange juice, remaining tablespoon of vinegar, the honey, and remaining 2 tablespoons of oil together in a bowl. Season.

When the squash is cooked, set aside. Bring a large pan of water to a boil. Break an egg into a small bowl, then slip into the boiling water. Repeat with the remaining eggs. Poach for 3 minutes, or until the whites are set and the yolks are runny. Drain on a plate lined with a paper towel.

Add the broccoli to the squash and drizzle over half the dressing. Serve with the nuts, chervil, poached egg, and remaining dressing.

10 min. / 10–15 min.

Kale & quinoa patties

Makes: 8
3 tablespoons (45 ml) olive oil
1 onion, finely chopped
2 garlic cloves, crushed
1⅓ cups (250 g) cooked quinoa
1½ cups (100 g) kale, stems removed and leaves roughly chopped
1 cup (120 g) all-purpose flour
2 large eggs, beaten
1 teaspoon toasted cumin seeds
9 oz. (250 g) halloumi, grated
salt and pepper

To serve
⅔ cup (150 g) plain yogurt
3 tablespoons rose harissa paste
1 preserved lemon, finely chopped

Heat 1 tablespoon of the olive oil in a large nonstick frying pan over medium heat. Add the onion and fry for 2–3 minutes until translucent. Add the garlic and cook for another 1 minute. Tip the cooked quinoa into a bowl and add the kale, onion, garlic, flour, eggs, cumin seeds, and grated halloumi. Season well and mix to combine. Set aside.

Gently heat the remaining olive oil in a shallow skillet. Using your hands, form the quinoa mixture into 8 round patties. Add to the skillet and fry for 4–5 minutes on each side until crisp and golden. You will need to do this in 2 batches.

Mix the yogurt and harissa together in a bowl and serve with the warm patties for dunking. Sprinkle over the chopped preserved lemon and season generously.

10 min. / 20 min.

Black bean & kale soup with avocado & feta

Serves: 4

2 tablespoons olive oil
5 garlic cloves, chopped
1 large bunch of cilantro, stems finely chopped and leaves picked
2 limes
2 teaspoons ground cumin
2 tablespoons chipotle chili paste
2 x 14 oz. (400 g) cans chopped tomatoes
14 oz. (400 g) can black beans, rinsed and drained
4 cups (1 L) chicken broth
3 cups (200 g) kale, thick stems removed, leaves chopped
1¾ oz. (50 g) feta, crumbled
1 avocado, sliced

Heat the olive oil in a large pan, add the garlic, cilantro stems, and the juice and zest of 1 lime, and fry for 3 minutes. Stir in the cumin and chipotle chili paste and fry for another minute.

Add the chopped tomatoes, beans, and broth. Bring to a boil, then reduce the heat and simmer for 10 minutes. Using a potato masher, crush some of the beans into the base of the pan. This will thicken the soup.

Stir the kale into the soup and simmer for 3 minutes, or until wilted. Ladle into bowls and top with the cilantro leaves, feta, and sliced avocado. Serve with the remaining lime, quartered, on the side.

Kale & chickpea stew with coconut & spices

Serves: 4

½ cup (115 ml) olive oil

1 large onion, diced

5 garlic cloves, finely grated

2 tablespoons finely grated ginger

14 oz. (400 g) can chickpeas, drained and rinsed

2 teaspoons ground turmeric

1 teaspoon chili pepper flakes

13.5 oz. (400 ml) can coconut milk

4½ cups (300 g) green kale, stems removed and leaves chopped

To serve (optional)

plain yogurt

chopped red chili pepper

Heat the olive oil in a pan over medium heat, add the onion and fry for 10 minutes, stirring frequently so it doesn't stick. Increase the heat, add the garlic and ginger, and fry for another 2 minutes, then add the chickpeas and fry, tossing constantly, for 3 minutes.

Add the turmeric, chili pepper flakes, coconut milk, and 2 cups (500 ml) hot water or broth. Reduce the heat to low and simmer for 20 minutes, or until the soup has thickened and become creamy. Add the kale, cover with a lid, and cook for another 5 minutes. Serve in bowls, topped with a little yogurt and chopped chili pepper, if you like.

broccoli

Broccoli comes from the Italian word *broccolo* and means "the flowering crest of a cabbage." The head and stems can be eaten. It is a cruciferous vegetable, which means it is in the same family as cabbage, kale, and cauliflower.

what's in it?

1 cup (90 g) raw broccoli is made up of nearly 90% water, 7% carbs, 3% protein, and no fat. It is cholesterol free, gluten free, and a good source of plant-based calcium. It contains:

- Just 31 calories
- Full daily requirement of vitamin K (90 mcg)
- 81 mcg vitamin C, well above the daily recommended intake of 60 mcg

- High levels of iron, folate, potassium, and manganese
- Antioxidants and plant compounds, namely sulforaphane
- Fiber

what can it do for me?

The high sulforaphane content in broccoli is thought to reduce the risk of cancer. In research, sulforaphane reduced the size of a number of cancer cells and blocked further tumor growth. The fiber in broccoli is known to promote digestion and bowel health as well as regulate blood sugar levels.

how to eat broccoli

Broccoli is very versatile. You can eat it raw, roasted, steamed, or fried. It can be used in soups and blended or even juiced. Avoid overcooking broccoli as it will turn mushy and reduce the availability of the vitamins and minerals.

varieties

Depending on the climate and where you want to grow broccoli, there are lots of varieties of the green-headed broccoli. They mostly vary by the size of the head, sprouting color, and leaf.

GREEN HEAD BROCCOLI—many heirloom varieties (Belstar, Calabrese, Destiny, Di Cicco, Green Goliath, Green Magic, Sun King, Waltham 29)

PURPLE SPROUTING

BROCCOLI RAAB

BROCCOLINI

how to cook broccoli

type of veg	quantity for 2	quantity for 4	cooking vessel	quantity of liquid	salt	oil / butter

steam

type of veg	quantity for 2	quantity for 4	cooking vessel	quantity of liquid	salt	oil / butter
Broccoli	½ head		↑	↑	↑	1 tablespoon olive oil or butter
Purple Sprouting Broccoli	2¼ cups (200 g)		steamer	¾ inch (2 cm) water in steamer	1 teaspoon	1 tablespoon olive oil or butter
Broccolini	2¼ cups (200 g)		↓	↓	↓	1 tablespoon sesame oil

bake/roast

type of veg	quantity for 2	quantity for 4	cooking vessel	quantity of liquid	salt	oil / butter
Broccoli	↑		↑		↑	1 tablespoon vegetable oil
Purple Sprouting Broccoli	2¾ cups (250 g)		large flat baking sheet		1 teaspoon	1 tablespoon olive oil
Broccolini	↓		↓		↓	1 tablespoon coconut oil

fry

type of veg	quantity for 2	quantity for 4	cooking vessel	quantity of liquid	salt	oil / butter
Broccoli	↑		large skillet or griddle pan		1 teaspoon	1 tablespoon vegetable oil
Purple Sprouting Broccoli			large skillet or wok		1 teaspoon	1 tablespoon vegetable oil
Broccolini	3¼ cups (300 g)		large skillet or wok			1–2 tablespoons vegetable oil
	↓					

soup

type of veg	quantity for 2	quantity for 4	cooking vessel	quantity of liquid	salt	oil / butter
Broccoli		↑	↑	↑	↑	↑
Purple Sprouting Broccoli		1 large head of broccoli	large deep saucepan	4 cups (1 L) broth	1 teaspoon	1 tablespoon olive oil
		↓	↓	↓	↓	↓

rice

type of veg	quantity for 2	quantity for 4	cooking vessel	quantity of liquid	salt	oil / butter
Broccoli		1 large head of broccoli				
Purple Sprouting Broccoli						

other ingredients	heat	with lid	cooking time	notes
3 garlic cloves, chopped, juice of ½ lemon	↑	↑	4–5 min.	Steam broccoli until tender. Toss with oil, garlic, and lemon for a side.
juice of 1 lemon, toasted hazelnuts	medium	yes	4 min.	Trim off the thickest part of the stem if it seems woody and tough.
sesame seeds, 3 garlic cloves, sliced, 1 chili pepper, diced	↓	↓	3 min.	Should be a vibrant green and tender when cooked.
grated zest and juice of ½ lemon	400°F (200°C)	↑	30 min.	Toss the broccoli in the oil, lemon juice, and zest. Season. Roast.
1 tablespoon balsamic vinegar, 2 garlic cloves, chopped, handful of toasted pine nuts	425°F (220°C)	no	15–18 min.	Cooking broccoli at a slightly lower temperature will allow the stems to get tender and the florets to begin to crisp up.
1 tablespoon each soy sauce, vinegar, garlic, and ginger	475°F (250°C)	↓	15 min.	Mix additional ingredients with the oil and toss with broccoli; roast.
chopped garlic, breadcrumbs	↑		6 min.	Heat a griddle over high heat and char broccoli for 3 min. on each side.
chopped ginger, sesame seeds, lime			6 min.	As above.
chopped garlic, chopped ginger, sliced red chili pepper, scallions, lime, honey, soy sauce	high		7 min.	Place the pan over high heat and get very hot before adding ingredients. If using aromatics such as garlic and ginger, briefly fry these off in a little oil before adding trimmed broccoli.
	↓			
↑	↑	↑	↑	Heat the oil in the pan and fry the veg until soft. Add the broccoli and broth. Season. Simmer for 10–15 min. until broccoli is tender, then purée until smooth. Finish with cream or yogurt.
1 leek, 1 celery stick, 2 garlic cloves, cream or yogurt to drizzle at end	medium	no	10–15 min.	
↓	↓	↓	↓	
while not strictly needed, consider adding complementary flavors, such as chopped soft herbs, ground spices, or lemon zest				Pulse chopped broccoli in a food processor to resemble rice.

PREP / COOK TIME

TIP

vegan / gluten-free

10 min. / 15 min.

Serve this simple broccoli dish alongside steamed or broiled fish, or meat and fluffy rice.

Crispy Asian-style broccoli

Serves: 4 as a side

5½ cups (500 g) broccolini, woody ends removed and large stems sliced in half

2 tablespoons coconut oil, melted

4 tablespoons tamari

4 tablespoons seasoned rice vinegar

1 tablespoon sriracha chili sauce

3 garlic cloves, finely sliced

2½–3½-inch (6–9 cm) piece of ginger, peeled and sliced into matchsticks

1 tablespoon toasted sesame seeds

chopped red chili pepper, to garnish (optional)

Preheat the oven to 475°F (250°C) or as hot as your oven will go.

Place the broccoli in a single layer on a large baking sheet.

In a small bowl, whisk together the melted oil, tamari, vinegar, sriracha, garlic, and ginger. Pour over the broccoli and toss until thoroughly combined.

Bake for 10 minutes, then turn the broccoli over and bake for another 5 minutes until the heads become crispy and sticky. Finish with sesame seeds and a little chopped chili pepper, if you like.

15 min. / 0 min.

Raw broccoli slaw

**Serves: 2 as a main,
4 as a side**

1 red onion, sliced in half
2 lemons
1 head broccoli,
broken into small florets
½ cup (112 g) Greek
yogurt
2 tablespoons rose
harissa paste
½ bunch of mint,
leaves picked
1 tablespoon toasted
cumin seeds
salt and pepper

Using a mandoline with a gate on, carefully shave the onion into very thin half-moons and place on a large platter. Squeeze the juice of 1 lemon over the top and season well with salt. Set aside. Do the same with the broccoli. You want to aim for 1/16-inch (2 mm) thick slivers. Toss the broccoli in with the onions.

Mix the yogurt, harissa, and juice and zest of the remaining lemon together in a bowl. You may need 1 tablespoon water depending on how juicy the lemon is. Season well with salt and pepper and toss through the slaw. Finish with mint leaves and cumin seeds.

Thai-style broccoli rice

Serves: 2

⅔ cup (100 g) peanuts
1 head broccoli, cut into
florets and the stem cut
in half
2 tablespoons light
coconut oil
1 red onion, finely diced
1 bunch of cilantro
with roots, roots finely
chopped, leaves whole
3 garlic cloves, crushed
2½–3½-inch (6–9 cm)
piece of ginger, peeled
and grated
1 red chili pepper,
finely diced

Dressing
grated zest and juice
of 1 lime
2 tablespoons tamari
1½ teaspoons light
brown sugar
2 tablespoons peanut oil

Heat a skillet over medium heat and add the peanuts. Toast evenly, regularly shaking the pan, then remove and set aside.

Place the broccoli in a food processor and pulse until it looks like green couscous. Transfer to a large bowl and set aside.

Make the dressing by whisking the lime zest and juice, tamari, sugar, and peanut oil together in a bowl until combined. Set aside.

Heat the coconut oil in a large nonstick skillet, add the onion, cilantro roots, garlic, ginger, and chili pepper and fry until soft and aromatic. Add the broccoli rice to the pan and toss through. Fry for 4–5 minutes until it still has a little bite. Turn off the heat and mix through half the cilantro leaves and half the toasted peanuts.

Toss the dressing through the broccoli rice and tip onto a serving plate. Sprinkle over the remaining peanuts and cilantro leaves. Serve hot.

Charred broccoli & romesco salad

Serves: 4

6 tablespoons (90 ml) olive oil, plus extra for drizzling

3½ oz. (100 g) sourdough bread

½ cup (190 g) jarred roasted red bell peppers, drained

2 large garlic cloves

½ cup (60 g) blanched almonds

½ bunch of flat-leaf parsley, a handful of leaves kept for the end

2 tablespoons red wine vinegar

1 teaspoon smoked paprika

salt

5½ cups (500 g) broccolini, woody ends trimmed

Pour half the olive oil into a large skillet and tear in the slices of bread. You are aiming for random bite-sized pieces. Toss all the bread in the oil and place over medium heat. Fry the bread for 6 minutes, or until crisp and golden all over. Remove from the pan and place on a plate.

Add the red bell peppers, garlic, almonds, parsley leaves and stems, vinegar, paprika, the remaining olive oil, and a handful of the toasted bread to a blender. Season well with salt and blend until smooth.

Heat a large griddle pan over high heat, drizzle a little olive oil over the broccolini, and char for 3 minutes on each side. You may need to do this in batches.

Smear the romesco sauce over a large platter or serving plates and top with the broccoli and remaining toasted bread. Finish with a drizzle of olive oil and sprinkle over the reserved parsley leaves.

Serve this simple frittata with a light green salad and a dollop of Dijon mustard for a summer lunch, if you like.

Blue cheese & broccoli frittata

Serves: 4

2¼ cups (200 g) purple sprouting broccoli
½ bunch of flat-leaf parsley, leaves picked and stems finely chopped
8 large eggs
⅓ cup (50 g) pine nuts
1 red chili pepper, chopped
3½ oz. (100 g) blue cheese, e.g., Gorgonzola, Roquefort, or Maytag Blue
½ cup (50 g) grated Parmesan cheese
½ cup (113 g) unsalted butter
salt and pepper
extra virgin olive oil

Preheat the oven to 425°F (220°C).

Cut off the broccoli florets and slice the stems into ⅓-inch (1 cm) strips. Toss the florets and stems in a little olive oil, then place on a griddle pan over high heat and cook for about 6 minutes, or until charred all over. Set aside in a bowl with the parsley stems.

Break the eggs into a large bowl and season well with salt and pepper. Stir through the pine nuts and chopped chili pepper. Crumble in the blue cheese, then add the grated Parmesan. Toss through the broccoli with the parsley leaves.

Melt the butter with a splash of olive oil in a an 8-inch (20 cm) oven-safe skillet and place over medium heat. Pour in the egg mix and cook for 2–3 minutes until the bottom starts to set slightly. Place the pan in the oven for 8–10 minutes until the frittata is puffed up, golden, and almost set. Serve hot or warm.

10 min. / 20 min.

Roasted purple sprouting broccoli with yogurt & preserved lemons

Serves: 2

3¼ cups (300 g) purple sprouting broccoli, stems trimmed

4 tablespoons (60 ml) olive oil

3 garlic cloves, finely sliced

1 tablespoon Turkish chili pepper flakes (Aleppo pepper)

1 preserved lemon, finely chopped

½ cup (100 g) Greek yogurt

2 tablespoons tahini

1 tablespoon finely chopped flat-leaf parsley

salt and pepper

Preheat the oven to 475°F (250°C).

Arrange the broccoli over a large baking sheet. You may need to use 2 trays. Toss well with half the olive oil and the sliced garlic. Season well with salt and pepper and roast for 10 minutes.

After 10 minutes, sprinkle the chili pepper flakes over the broccoli and toss well. Return to the oven for another 8–10 minutes until crunchy.

Meanwhile, mix the preserved lemon with the yogurt, tahini, parsley, and enough cold water to make it a good runny consistency. Finish with the remaining olive oil. Season well with salt and pepper and drizzle over most of the broccoli. Serve with the remaining dressing on the side.

Fennel sausage & broccoli pizza

TIP

This pizza is flavorful and a brilliant way of hiding vegetables from the kids. Play around with your favorite toppings.

Makes: 1 large pizza

PREP / COOK TIME:
10 min. / 30 min.

1 head broccoli
⅔ cup (100 g) ground almonds
1¼ cups (100 g) rolled oats
pinch of dried oregano

2 eggs, beaten
olive oil
4 tablespoons passata
3 Italian fennel sausages, removed from casings

1 garlic clove, sliced
1 ball of fresh mozzarella
1 handful of basil leaves
salt and pepper

01 Preheat the oven to 425°F (220°C). Pulse the broccoli in a food processor to a rice-like texture. Place in a bowl, add the ground almonds, oats, and oregano. Season. Mix, then make a well in the center and add the eggs.

02 Mix everything together, then use your hands to form the mixture into a ball. It will be a little wetter and less firm than a traditional pizza dough.

03 Line a baking sheet with parchment paper, then rub it with olive oil. Place the dough in the middle and flatten it out until it is about ¼ inch (5 mm) thick—slightly thicker around the edges. Bake for 20 minutes, or until just golden.

04 Increase the oven temperature to 475°F (250°C). Spread the passata over the base. Add the sausage, in pieces, sliced garlic, and tear over the mozzarella. Bake for 10 minutes. Drizzle with olive oil and sprinkle over the basil.

peas

The pea is known to be both the small round green edible seed and the green pod of the fruit. Botanically, pea pods are fruits since they contain seeds. Each pod contains several peas, which can be green or yellow. The immature peas as well as the pods in some varieties are used as a vegetable, and the tendrils of the climbing plant are also often consumed.

what's in them?

Peas are sweet and starchy and are a good source of plant-based protein, which makes them filling to eat. 1 cup (160 g) cooked peas contains:

- 134 calories
- 8 g fiber
- 8 g protein
- High levels of vitamins A, K, and C

- Several minerals including folate, manganese, iron, and phosphorus
- Polyphenol antioxidant
- A phytochemical called saponin

what can peas do for me?

The high fiber content of peas supports good bacteria in the gut to maintain a healthy digestive tract and bowel health. The combination of high fiber and protein are shown to regulate blood sugar levels, which is helpful for people with type 2 diabetes, as well as helping to reduce the risk of diabetes and heart disease. The saponins are thought to provide antioxidant and anti-cancer benefits.

how to eat peas

Peas are eaten and cooked in a variety of ways. Eat raw and fresh, frozen, and canned. Some varieties are dried and rehydrated when cooked in dal and soups. Peas are commonly added to dishes such as pasta, curries, and quiches to boost their nutritional value, but they can also be used to make soups and salads in which they are the main ingredient of the dish.

varieties

Aside from English garden peas, there are a number of other varieties of peas, which are regularly used in many cuisines:

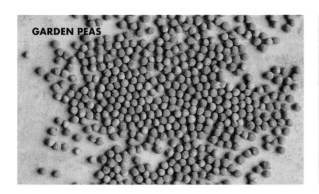

GARDEN PEAS

SUGAR SNAP PEAS

SNOW PEAS

LINCOLN

other varieties

Here are some less common varieties of peas are grown:

- **TALL TELEPHONE**: This is a tall variety of pea and needs to be grown up a support. It is a great pea for the home gardener and flowers over a long period of time, allowing for lots of pickings

- **MAESTRO**: An heirloom variety of pea, it is used in the kitchen as a shelling pea

- **GREEN ARROW**: This is an early spring and fall variety, which is perfect for shelling and eating fresh

how to cook peas

type of veg	quantity for 2	quantity for 4	cooking vessel	quantity of liquid	salt	oil / butter

steam

type of veg	quantity for 2	quantity for 4	cooking vessel	quantity of liquid	salt	oil / butter
Peas	1¼ cups (180 g)		↑	↑	↑	↑
Sugar Snap Peas	1⅓ cups (150 g)		steamer	¾ inch (2 cm) water in steamer	1 teaspoon	1 tablespoon oil or butter
Snow Peas	1¼ cups (150 g)		↓	↓	↓	↓

bake/roast

type of veg	quantity for 2	quantity for 4	cooking vessel	quantity of liquid	salt	oil / butter
Peas	1⅓ cups (200 g)		↑		↑	2 tablespoons butter 1 tablespoon olive oil
Sugar Snap Peas	1⅔ cups (200 g)		medium baking sheet		1 teaspoon	
			↓		↓	

fry

type of veg	quantity for 2	quantity for 4	cooking vessel	quantity of liquid	salt	oil / butter
Peas	1¼ cups (180 g)		large nonstick skillet		↑	↑
Sugar Snap Peas	1½ cup (180 g)		large nonstick skillet		1 teaspoon	1 tablespoon butter or olive oil
Snow Peas	1¼ cup (150 g)		large cast-iron or nonstick skillet		↓	↓

soup

type of veg	quantity for 2	quantity for 4	cooking vessel	quantity of liquid	salt	oil / butter
↑ Peas ↓		↑ 3⅓ cups (600 g) peas ↓	↑ large deep saucepan ↓	↑ 3¾ cups (900 ml) good-quality broth ↓	↑ 1 teaspoon ↓	↑ 1 tablespoon oil or butter ↓

other ingredients	heat	with lid	cooking time	notes
↑	↑	↑	2–3 min.	Steam fresh or frozen peas; if fresh they should only take 1–2 min.
2 scallions, mint leaves, feta	medium	yes	4 min.	Best served with knob of butter and seasoned well.
↓	↓	↓	3 min.	Should still have a bite when cooked, great served with other greens in a bean salad with green beans and sugar snaps for a variety of textures.
4 garlic cloves, smashed in their skins	350°F (180°C)	↑	20–25 min.	Melt butter and toss with peas and garlic. Bake until golden.
1 lemon, quartered; freshly cracked black pepper	425°F (220°C)	no	20 min.	Toss sugar snaps with oil, add lemon juice, and bake with lemon quarters, tossing after 10 min.
		↓		
2 garlic cloves, minced; mustard seeds; lemon zest; cayenne	medium-high	↑	3–5 min.	Heat oil or butter in a pan, add garlic, and fry until soft and fragrant. Add spices, peas and cook for 3–5 min.
chopped mint, lemon zest and juice	medium-high	no	2–3 min.	When in peak season, sugar snap peas are delicious raw, but a quick flash in a hot pan can help to tenderize and bring out the sweetness when they're slightly older.
toasted hazelnuts, roughly chopped; zest and juice of lemon or orange; tarragon, chopped	high	↓	2–3 min.	Quickly cooked with either a lashing of butter or a splash of olive oil, snow peas become sweet and tender with the addition of a little heat.
↑ 1 onion, chopped; 1 garlic clove, chopped; mint, chopped; heavy cream to finish ↓	↑ medium ↓	↑ no ↓	↑ 10–15 min. ↓	Heat oil in the pan and sauté chopped onion and garlic until soft. Add frozen peas and broth and season. Simmer for 10 minutes until peas are tender. Take off heat, add a large handful of chopped mint and a few tablespoons cream, then blend until smooth.

TIP

This is the perfect way to use peas. It is very simple and fresh, perfect for a starter or a light lunch with some charred sourdough.

Pea & pea shoot burrata salad

Serves: 2

2 cups (300 g) peas (fresh or frozen)

grated zest and juice of 1 lemon

1 green chili pepper, finely chopped

3 tablespoons (50 ml) olive oil

½ bunch of mint, leaves picked

½ bunch of basil, leaves picked

2 balls of baby burrata

2 cups (200 g) pea shoots

extra virgin olive oil, for drizzling

salt

Half-fill a medium saucepan with water, add a little salt, and bring to a rolling boil. Add the peas and cook for 2 minutes, or until they float and are bright green. Drain in a sieve and rinse under cold running water until cold.

Set aside 3 tablespoons of the cooked peas and add the rest of them to a blender along with the lemon juice and zest, chili pepper, olive oil, and half the herb leaves. Blend to a smooth purée.

Smear the pea purée over plates or in a serving bowl, top with the burrata, sprinkle over the pea shoots, remaining herbs and peas, then drizzle with a little extra olive oil.

TIP

gluten-free

Peas are at their best in the summer, so try to find fresh ones. This soup is usually served cold, but it is also delicious hot with some crusty white bread.

Pea & chervil soup with crispy pancetta

Serves: 4

1 tablespoon olive oil
4 shallots, roughly chopped
2 garlic cloves, sliced
5¼ cups (700 g) frozen peas
4 cups (1 L) chicken or vegetable broth
½ bunch of chervil
1¾ oz. (50 g) pancetta, sliced
2 tablespoons crème fraîche or sour cream
extra virgin olive oil, for drizzling
salt and pepper

Place a large saucepan over medium heat, add the olive oil, shallots, and garlic and fry for 5 minutes, or until softened. Add the peas, pour in the broth, and bring to a simmer. Cook for 5 minutes.

Add most of the chervil to the pan, keeping a handful for the top, then purée with a handheld blender until very smooth. Season to taste, then let cool for 2 hours, or overnight, if you like.

Preheat the oven to 400°F (200°C).

Lay the slices of pancetta over a baking sheet and place in the oven for 3 minutes. Turn them over and return to the oven for another 1 minute, or until crispy.

Ladle the chilled soup into bowls, crumble over the crispy pancetta, add a dollop of crème fraîche, a drizzle of extra virgin olive oil, and the reserved chervil leaves. If you like, add a few ice cubes to make it extra cooling.

PREP / COOK TIME

TIP

gluten-free / nut-free

10 min. / 10 min.

Serve these fish cakes with charred broccoli on page 56 or a light green salad for a simple midweek meal.

Pea & salmon fish cakes with miso

Serves: 4

2 lemongrass stalks

2½-inch (6 cm) piece of ginger, peeled and roughly chopped

1¼ cups (150 g) frozen peas

½ bunch of cilantro, leaves picked and stems chopped

1 lb. 2 oz. (500 g) salmon fillets, skin off, bones removed, and roughly chopped

2 limes, grated zest of 1 and juice of 2

8 tablespoons sesame seeds

1 tablespoon olive oil

2 teaspoons miso paste

Slice the lemongrass in half and slide off the outer layer. Roughly chop and add to a blender with the ginger, frozen peas, half the cilantro leaves, and all the stems and mix to a rough paste. Add half the salmon and blend until smooth. Add the remaining salmon and pulse so the mixture has some texture. Add the lime zest and season well.

Divide the mixture evenly into 4 portions, then shape and squash each portion into 1¼-inch (3 cm) thick patties. Pour the sesame seeds onto a plate and sprinkle over all sides of the patties until coated.

Heat the olive oil in a large skillet over medium-high heat. Add the patties and fry for 3 minutes on each side until golden.

Mix the miso and lime juice together in a bowl, then spoon half over the fish cakes and fry for another 1 minute. Serve the fish cakes with any remaining dressing and the rest of the cilantro leaves.

10 min. / 45 min.

Serve this dish with steamed basmati rice and fresh naans for a comforting meal, or serve alongside the paneer curry on page 18 and the Indian spinach salad on page 24 for a real feast.

Keema peas

Serves: 4

2 tablespoons ghee
2 onions, finely sliced
5 garlic cloves, crushed
2 teaspoons hot chili powder
2 tablespoons garam masala
2-inch (5 cm) piece of ginger, peeled and grated
1 lb. (450 g) lean ground beef
14 oz. (400 g) can chopped tomatoes
1⅔ cups (200 g) frozen peas
6½ cups (200 g) spinach
⅔ cup (150 g) plain yogurt
1 large handful of cilantro leaves
juice of 1 lime
salt and pepper
lime wedges, to serve

Heat the ghee in a large skillet over medium heat. Add the onions and fry for 8–10 minutes until soft and reduced. Add the garlic and fry for another 3 minutes. Add the chili powder, garam masala, and grated ginger and fry for 2–3 minutes. Transfer the onion mixture to a bowl and increase the heat. Add the beef to the pan and fry for 3–4 minutes, breaking it all apart with a wooden spoon. Add the chopped tomatoes and the reserved onion mixture, then pour in 1 cup (250 ml) boiling water and simmer for 20 minutes, stirring occasionally.

Add the peas and spinach, then cook for 4 minutes, or until the peas are soft and the spinach has wilted.

Stir in ½ cup (100 g) of the yogurt, a large handful of cilantro leaves, and the lime juice. Taste and season with salt and pepper. Top with the remaining yogurt and cilantro. Serve with lime wedges.

10 min. / 35 min.

Pea & asparagus quick tart

Serves: 4

11½ oz. (320 g) puff pastry

1 egg, beaten

2¼ cups (200 g) chopped Swiss chard, leaves and stems separated

7 oz. (200 g) goat cheese

½ cup (100 g) frozen peas

14 oz. (400 g) asparagus, woody ends removed

1 bunch of flat-leaf parsley, leaves picked and stems chopped

½ cup (115 ml) olive oil

Preheat the oven to 400°F (200°C). Line a large baking sheet with parchment paper.

Unroll the pastry, then roll it out a little wider and lay on the prepared baking sheet. Using a sharp knife, score a border about ¾ inch (2 cm) in from the edge, making sure you don't cut all the way through. Prick the central area with a fork and glaze the border with the beaten egg. Bake in the oven for 10–15 minutes until golden and almost cooked.

Meanwhile, simmer the chard stems in a large pan of salted water for 1 minute. Add the leaves and cook for another 30 seconds, or until barely cooked. Drain, refresh in cold water, then drain again. Transfer to a clean dish towel and squeeze out any excess water. Remove the pastry from the oven and flatten the center with the back of a spoon. Arrange the chard, goat cheese, frozen peas, and asparagus over the center. Bake for 10–15 minutes until the tart is crisp and golden.

Place the parsley and stems with the olive oil in a blender. Season and blend until it is a vivid green oil.

Remove the tart from the oven and spoon over the parsley oil before serving immediately.

Wasabi peas

TIP

Store these in an airtight jar in a cool place for up to 12 months for a quick snack. You can also add these to salads for some crunch or in poke bowls for flavor and color.

vegan / gluten-free / nut-free

Makes: 4 cups (400 g)
PREP / COOK TIME: 12 hr. / 5 hr.

3 cups (600 g) dried whole peas
2 tablespoons olive oil

4 teaspoons wasabi powder
2 tablespoons tahini

2 tablespoons rice vinegar
2 teaspoons Dijon mustard

01 Soak the peas in 3 times the amount of water overnight or for at least 12 hours. Preheat the oven to 325°F (160°C).

02 Drain the peas, place in a large pan of water, and bring to a boil. Reduce the heat and simmer for 40 minutes, or until the peas are a little tender. Drain in a colander and mix with the olive oil until well coated.

03 Spread the peas evenly across a large roasting pan and bake in the oven for 4 hours, or until the peas appear dry and are crisp. You will need to toss the pan about every hour or so. Increase the oven temperature to 475°F (250°C).

04 Mix the wasabi powder, tahini, vinegar, mustard, and 2 tablespoons water together until it is a runny paste. Tip in the peas and mix until they are well coated. Tip the peas back in the pan and bake for 10–15 minutes until crisp.

sweet potatoes

Sweet potatoes are a flowering vine with an underground tuber forming the root vegetables that we commonly eat. Sweet potatoes are in the morning glory family and are not in the same family group as other root vegetables or potatoes.

what's in them?

There is only a small variation in micronutrient density of sweet potatoes when cooked compared to raw. 1 cup (130 g) raw sweet potatoes contains:

- 103 calories
- 0 g fat
- 24 g carbohydrates, including 4 g fiber
- 2.3 g protein
- Well over 100% of your daily recommended intake of vitamin A
- One-quarter of your daily needs for vitamins C and B6
- High quantities of potassium, calcium, iron, folate, and manganese
- Quercetin, a flavonoid antioxidant with anti-inflammatory properties

what can they do for me?

Sweet potatoes may benefit people with diabetes as they are high in fiber and so can regulate blood sugar levels and assist in maintaining a healthy blood pressure.

how to eat sweet potatoes

The simplest way to eat a sweet potato is to bake it in its skin. While it is generally cooked, steamed, roasted, or fried, sweet potatoes can also be eaten raw in a juice or added to a smoothie. Keep the skin on as it contributes to the amounts of fiber you benefit from.

varieties

Sweet potato varieties can be difficult to differentiate, and yams, although similar, are from a different family. Differences in skin and inside color and texture, as well as how the potato cooks, are good ways to tell varieties apart.

PINK SKIN

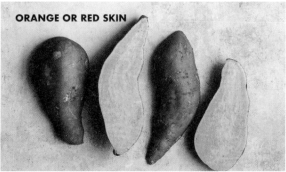

ORANGE OR RED SKIN

PURPLE SKIN

WHITE SWEET POTATOES

other varieties

Here are some less common varieties of sweet potatoes that are grown:

- **YELLOW SWEET POTATOES**: This sweet potato is common in the US and has a golden skin and a creamy white flesh

- **OKINAWAN SWEET POTATOES:** Also known as Hawaiian sweet potato, this has a tubular shape with purple flesh

- **BONIATO**: This sweet potato looks like a yam as it has dry white flesh and pink skin; it is one of the most popular sweet potatoes in the Caribbean

how to cook sweet

type of veg	quantity for 2	quantity for 4	cooking vessel	quantity of liquid	salt	oil / butter

steam

Sweet Potatoes	2 sweet potatoes		steamer	2 inch (5 cm) water in steamer	½ tablespoon	2 tablespoons butter

bake/roast

Sweet Potatoes	2 sweet potatoes		small baking sheet		1 teaspoon	1 tablespoon olive oil

fry

Sweet Potatoes	1–2 sweet potatoes		large cast-iron or nonstick skillet	5–6 tablespoons broth or water	1 teaspoon	3 tablespoons either

soup

Sweet potatoes		1 lb. 11 oz. (750 g)	large deep saucepan	6⅓ cups (1.5 L) broth	1 teaspoon	1 tablespoon olive oil

potatoes

other ingredients	heat	with lid	cooking time	notes
butter, sesame seeds, juice of 1 lime	medium	yes	25–30 min.	Scrub skins of sweet potatoes before steaming until fork-tender. Split open and serve with generous lashings of butter, some sesame seeds, and the juice of a lime.
	350°F (180°C)	no	40 min.	You can easily bake sweet potatoes much faster than regular potatoes for a very quick weeknight side. Rub with oil and salt and bake on a pan for 40 minutes until tender. You can also peel and chop the sweet potatoes to make wedges or fries.
thyme sprigs; 1 garlic clove, bashed; cinnamon stick	medium-low	yes	15–20 min.	Harder root vegetables, such as sweet potato, are more commonly roasted but produce great results when cooked on the stove. The key to cooking these harder vegetables in a pan is to regulate the temperature so they cook through without burning on the outside. Sliced into thick rounds, they can be browned on both sides with oil or butter and salt before adding a small amount of liquid—either broth or water—and some aromatics, such as thyme, a whole bashed garlic clove, and cinnamon. Cover and cook over low heat until tender on the inside. Leave the skin on to help retain the shape and speed up your prep time. Or peel and dice the sweet potato and cook as you would for a potato hash.
1 onion, chopped; 1 garlic clove, chopped; soft herbs, such as parsley and cilantro	medium	no	20 min.	Heat the oil in the pan and sauté the onion and garlic until soft and translucent. Add the sweet potato and cook for 5 minutes. Add the broth and season. Simmer for 10–15 minutes until the sweet potato is tender, then blend until smooth. Finish by stirring through some finely chopped herbs.

15 min. / 15 min.

Asian-style sweet potato salad

Serves: 4

1 large sweet potato, peeled
2 tablespoons peanut oil
¾ lb. (300 g) ground turkey
8 garlic cloves, sliced
3½-inch (9 cm) piece of ginger, peeled and sliced into matchsticks
1 tablespoon five-spice powder
⅔ cup (100 g) green beans, sliced
1 cup (150 g) cherry tomatoes, halved
1 bunch of Thai basil, leaves picked

Dressing

grated zest and juice of 3 limes
2 tablespoons fish sauce
2 tablespoons soy sauce
2 tablespoons toasted sesame oil

Using a julienne peeler or a spiralizer, peel long noodle shapes from the sweet potato. Add to a bowl with the dressing ingredients.

Place a large wok over high heat and heat for 2 minutes. Add the peanut oil and ground turkey and cook for 8 minutes, breaking the turkey up with a wooden spoon, until it starts to crisp and brown all over. Add the garlic, ginger, and five-spice and keep tossing it around for another 5 minutes. Everything should be crispy and golden. Remove from the heat and set aside.

Add the sweet potato noodles and dressing to a large platter. Add the turkey, then sprinkle over the green beans and tomato halves. Finish with the basil leaves.

PREP / COOK TIME

TIP

vegetarian / nut-free

10 min. / 20 min.

For vegans, simply leave out the eggs and serve with a little crispy tofu.

Sweet potato rosti with a fried egg & roasted tomatoes

Serves: 2

1 ⅓ cups (200 g) cherry tomatoes, sliced in half

3 tablespoons (45 ml) olive oil

salt and pepper

1 corn cob, husked and kernels cut from cob

2 ¼ cups (300 g) sweet potatoes, peeled and coarsely grated

½ bunch of cilantro, leaves picked and stems finely sliced

3 large eggs

1 teaspoon smoked paprika

3 tablespoons all-purpose flour

juice of 1 lime

Preheat the broiler to high.

Add the tomatoes to a small roasting pan with 1 tablespoon of the olive oil and season well. Broil, tossing every few minutes so the tomatoes evenly char. Set aside.

Place the corn kernels in a large bowl with the grated sweet potatoes and cilantro stems. Beat 1 of the eggs with the paprika, then season. Sprinkle the flour over the sweet potatoes mixture, add the beaten egg, and mix together with your hands.

Preheat a large skillet with 1 tablespoon of the olive oil. Divide the rosti mixture into 4 portions and squeeze between your hands to make loose patties. Place them in the pan and flatten slightly. Fry over medium heat for 8–10 minutes, turning once until golden on one side. Remove and set aside. Add the rest of the oil to the pan and fry the remaining eggs to your liking.

Serve the rostis topped with the fried eggs, tomatoes, lime juice, pepper, and cilantro leaves.

Sweet potato gnocchi with sage & pecorino

TIP

vegetarian / nut-free

Serve with grated pecorino. For a meat lover, serve with some crispy pancetta for a more indulgent dinner.

Serves: 4

PREP / COOK TIME:
15 min. / 15 min.

1 lb. (450 g) sweet potato
½ cup (100 g) ricotta
¾ cup (90 g) all-purpose flour, plus extra for dusting

⅔ cup (150 g) unsalted butter
1 bunch of sage

grated zest of 1 lemon
salt and pepper

01 Stab the sweet potato all over with a fork, run under a tap, and microwave on high for 12 minutes, or until very soft. When the sweet potato is cool enough to handle, scoop out the flesh, then mash into a bowl.

02 Stir in the ricotta, season, then sprinkle the flour into the mixture. Mix with a fork until a loose dough forms. Tip the dough onto a floured surface and knead 10 times, turning it 90 degrees each time until it is no longer sticky.

03 Divide the dough into 3 pieces and roll them into balls. Roll 1 ball of dough into an 8-inch (20 cm) long, 1-inch (2.5 cm) thick log. Cut the dough crossways into 12 x 1-inch (2.5 cm) pieces. Repeat to form 36 gnocchi. Cook in a pan of boiling water for 3–4 minutes.

04 Melt the butter and when the foam subsides, add the sage and lemon zest and cook until the sage is crispy and the butter is browned, about 3 minutes. Drain the gnocchi, add to the skillet, and toss to coat. Serve.

15 min. / 25 min.

Mexican sweet potato soup

Serves: 4

1 tablespoon olive oil

2 red onions, finely chopped

1 bunch of cilantro, leaves picked and stems chopped

2 tablespoons chipotle chili paste

5¾ cups (750 g) sweet potatoes, peeled and grated

6⅓ cups (1.5 L) vegetable broth

2 limes

salt

1 avocado, sliced

Heat the olive oil over medium heat in a large saucepan and fry three-quarters of the onion and the cilantro stems for 4–5 minutes until just soft. Stir in the chipotle chili paste and sweet potatoes and cook for another 5 minutes.

Add the broth to the pan along with the juice of 1 lime. Bring to a boil, then cover, reduce the heat, and simmer for 15 minutes until the sweet potatoes are soft. Add half the cilantro leaves and blend with a handheld blender until smooth.

Meanwhile, add the remaining onion to a bowl with the juice of the remaining lime. Season with salt and mix thoroughly. Set aside.

Once the soup is ready, taste and adjust the seasoning. Ladle the soup into bowls and serve with the remaining cilantro leaves, onions, and sliced avocado.

15 min. / 50 min.

Sweet potato & feta muffins

Makes: 12 muffins

2¼ cups (300 g) sweet potatoes, peeled and roughly grated

2 red chili peppers, finely sliced

½ cup (50 g) grated Parmesan cheese

3 large eggs

3 tablespoons cottage cheese

1 cup (125 g) whole-wheat self-rising flour

¼ cup (50 g) cooked black quinoa

3 tablespoons mixed seeds, such as pumpkin, sunflower, and sesame

Preheat the oven to 350°F (180°C). Line a 12-hole muffin pan with paper liners or 6-inch (15 cm) folded squares of parchment paper, then lightly wipe each one with oiled paper towel.

Place the sweet potatoes in a large bowl, add half the sliced chili peppers and most of the Parmesan with all the remaining ingredients, except the mixed seeds, and stir until well combined.

Evenly divide the mixture between the paper liners. Sprinkle over the mixed seeds, then dot over the reserved chili peppers. Lightly dust the remaining Parmesan over the top of each muffin and bake on the bottom shelf of the oven for 25–30 minutes until golden and set.

Polenta & rosemary sweet potato fries

Serves: 6 as a side

2¼ lb. (1 kg) sweet potatoes, peeled

7 tablespoons (100 ml) olive oil

2 teaspoons sweet smoked paprika

3 tablespoons fine polenta

1 head garlic, crushed with skins on

3 rosemary sprigs, leaves picked

sea salt

Preheat the oven to 400°F (200°C). Line 2 large baking sheet with parchment paper.

Cut the sweet potatoes into roughly ⅓ × 3-inch (1 × 8 cm) fries and place in a large bowl. Pour in 4 tablespoons (60 ml) of the olive oil and add the paprika and polenta. Toss until all the fries are evenly coated.

Divide the fries between the prepared baking sheet and roast for 15 minutes.

Meanwhile, add the garlic and rosemary leaves to a bowl and pour over the remaining olive oil. Season really well with salt.

After 15 minutes, toss the garlic mix through the fries, then return to the oven and continue to toss every 10 minutes for another 30 minutes, or until crispy and golden all over. Finish with a little extra sea salt and serve.

beets

Beets are the taproot section of a beet plant. They are one of several varieties of the *Beta vulgaris* plant from the Chenopodiaceae family. Beets have been used throughout history not just as a food but as a natural coloring and as a medicinal plant.

what's in them?

Beets are a rich source of vitamins and minerals. They consist mainly of water (87%), carbs (8%), and fiber (2–3%). 1 cup (190 g) boiled beets contains:

- 58 calories
- 1.6 g protein, 0.2 g fat
- Heart healthy nitrates
- Antioxidants, including alpha-lipoic acid and glutamine

- Calcium and vitamins C and B6
- 148 mcg folate
- 442 mg potassium

what can they do for me?

It has been found that drinking beet juice can lower blood pressure and enhance exercise performance. The high nitrate content is turned to nitric oxide in the body. This relaxes the artery walls and in turn dilates blood vessels and lowers blood pressure. Beets may also benefit people with diabetes and add to the health and maintenance of the intestinal tract.

how to eat beets

Both the root and the green leaves of beets are edible and are widely used. The natural sweetness of beets is brought out by roasting, however, beets are also often boiled, pickled, juiced, or eaten raw. They are a great addition to a salad, and their moisture and vibrant color make them great to use in baking too.

varieties

The varieties of beets make for a colorful array. The flavor differs as well as texture, but the color and shape are the main differences between beet types.

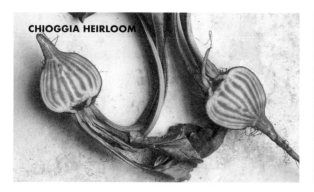

CHIOGGIA HEIRLOOM

BABY BEET

GOLDEN BEET

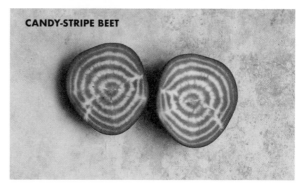

CANDY-STRIPE BEET

other varieties

Here are some less common varieties of beets that are grown:

- **WHITE BEETS**: This variety of beets does not bleed its color and has a sweet, mild flavor and a firm texture

how to cook beets

type of veg	quantity for 2	quantity for 4	cooking vessel	quantity of liquid	salt	oil / butter

steam

type of veg	quantity for 2	quantity for 4	cooking vessel	quantity of liquid	salt	oil / butter
Beets	9 oz. (250 g)		steamer	2 inches (5 cm) water in steamer	½ tablespoon	1 tablespoon olive oil

bake/roast

type of veg	quantity for 2	quantity for 4	cooking vessel	quantity of liquid	salt	oil / butter
Beets	2 beets		small baking sheet		1 teaspoon	1 tablespoon olive oil

fry

type of veg	quantity for 2	quantity for 4	cooking vessel	quantity of liquid	salt	oil / butter
Beets	9 oz. (250 g)		large cast-iron or nonstick skillet		1 teaspoon	1–2 tablespoons either

soup

type of veg	quantity for 2	quantity for 4	cooking vessel	quantity of liquid	salt	oil / butter
Beets		1 lb. 11 oz. (750 g)	deep saucepan or stockpot	6⅓ cups (1.5 L) good-quality broth	1 teaspoon	1 tablespoon olive oil

confit

type of veg	quantity for 2	quantity for 4	cooking vessel	quantity of liquid	salt	oil / butter
Beets		1 lb. 2 oz. (500 g)	deep baking dish		1 teaspoon	1 cup (250 ml) olive oil

other ingredients	heat	with lid	cooking time	notes
juice and zest of 1 orange, 1 teaspoon honey, mint leaves, 2 teaspoon toasted caraway seeds	↑ medium ↓	↑ yes ↓	↑ 45 min. ↓	Trim beets, but leave skin on and steam over salted water, topping up if necessary during cooking. Peel off skins once cooked. Combine olive oil, orange, and honey, then toss with mint and caraway.
	↑ 350°F (180°C) ↓	cover with foil	↑ 50 min. ↓	Trim off any leafy greens at the top. Wrap the oiled and salted beets in foil and roast for 50 min., or until tender and sweet. The skins should slide off once they are cooked.
splash of balsamic or sherry vinegar; 1 teaspoon honey or brown sugar; soft herbs, such as dill, parsley, thyme; walnuts, chopped	↑ medium ↓	↑ no ↓	↑ 8–10 min. ↓	Peel and dice the beets, heat the oil or butter in a pan and sauté the beets for a few minutes. Add the vinegar and sugar, and cook until tender. Stir through chopped herbs and walnuts to serve.
↑ 1 onion, finely chopped; 2 garlic cloves, chopped; sour cream; dill ↓	↑ medium ↓	↑ no ↓	↑ 20 min. ↓	Heat the oil in the pan and sauté the onion and garlic until soft. Add the finely diced or grated beets and cook for 5 min. Add the broth and season. Simmer for 10–15 min. until the beets are tender, then blend until smooth. Finish by topping with sour cream and dill.
↑ crushed garlic cloves, fennel seeds ↓	↑ 300°F (150°C) ↓	↑ no ↓	↑ 2–2½ hr. ↓	Use a baking dish that fits the beets snugly; nestle in the peeled beets and add the garlic cloves and fennel seeds. Season well with salt. The beets should be submerged at least halfway. Bake, turning halfway, until sticky and tender.

PREP / COOK TIME

15 min. / 45 min.

TIP

vegetarian / gluten-free

To make this salad vegan, use coconut or soy yogurt instead of the goat yogurt.

Whole roasted beets with beet top pesto

Serves: 4

12 mixed-color baby beets with leaves

¼ cup (60 ml) red wine vinegar

5 thyme sprigs

1 head garlic, peeled and cloves smashed

1 lemon

3 tablespoons (30 g) hazelnuts, toasted

½ cup (115 ml) olive oil

⅔ cup (150 g) goat yogurt

2 tablespoons dukkah

salt and pepper

Preheat the oven to 400°F (200°C).

Chop the leaves off the beets, discarding any rotten ones and keeping the small leaves to one side. Scrub the beets well, then place in a roasting pan. Add the vinegar, thyme, garlic, and peel in the skin of the lemon. Pour in ¼ cup (60 ml) water, then toss to coat. Season well, cover in foil, and roast for 45 minutes, tossing occasionally.

Meanwhile, add the reserved beet leaves to a blender, add the juice of the lemon, hazelnuts, olive oil, and season. Blend to a smooth oil.

Once the beets are ready, chop the large ones into quarters and the smaller ones in half or keep them whole.

Smear the goat yogurt over plates or a serving platter and top with the beets and all the extras from the pan. Sprinkle over the dukkah and top with a drizzle of the beet top pesto.

15 min. / 0 min.

Raw beet slaw

Serves: 4 as a side

5 raw mixed beets, peeled and cut into thin matchsticks
2 tablespoons tahini
grated zest and juice of 1 lemon
1 green chili pepper, chopped
2/3 cup (150 ml) buttermilk
1 bunch of cilantro, leaves picked
3/4 cup (100 g) pistachios, toasted and chopped
salt and pepper

Place the beets in a large bowl.

Mix the tahini, lemon zest and juice, chopped chili pepper, buttermilk, and a good pinch of salt and pepper together to make a silky dressing. You may need 1 tablespoon water depending on the thickness of your tahini. Taste and adjust the seasoning if needed.

Toss the dressing through the beets, then sprinkle over the cilantro and chopped pistachios.

15 min. / 45 min.

Beet & chocolate brownies

Makes: 12 brownies

1 cup (226 g) unsalted butter, cut into cubes, plus extra for greasing

9 oz. (250 g) beets, peeled and halved

9 oz. (250 g) dark chocolate (at least 70% cocoa solids), chopped into pieces

3 large eggs

1 teaspoon vanilla bean paste

1 cup (200 g) turbinado sugar

1¼ cups (150 g) self-rising flour

sea salt

Preheat the oven to 350°F (180°C). Grease an 8 × 10-inch (20 × 25 cm) brownie pan and line the base with parchment paper.

Place the beets in a pan, cover with water, and bring to a boil. Reduce the heat, cover, and simmer for 20 minutes, or until the beets feel soft when stabbed with a knife. Drain and leave to cool slightly. Once cool enough, coarsely grate on a box grater.

Place the butter and chocolate in a heatproof bowl set over a pan of simmering water. Make sure the base of the bowl doesn't touch the water, and stir until the mixture has melted.

Whisk the eggs, vanilla, and sugar together in a large bowl until combined, then beat in the melted chocolate mixture until smooth. Combine a pinch of salt with the flour, sift over the chocolate mixture, then fold in. Fold in the grated beets, then pour the batter into the pan and smooth the top. Bake for 25 minutes, or until a skewer inserted into the center comes out with a few moist crumbs clinging to it. Cool on a wire rack for 10 minutes in the pan, before cutting into 12 squares. Sprinkle with a little extra salt.

10 min. / 25 min.

Beet falafel

Makes: 20 balls

1 tablespoon olive oil, plus extra for brushing
1 onion, chopped
1 red chili pepper, diced
2 garlic cloves, chopped
2 teaspoons ground cumin
9 oz. (250 g) cooked beets
14 oz. (400 g) can chickpeas, drained and rinsed
2 cups (125 g) fresh white breadcrumbs
1 egg, beaten
sea salt

Preheat the oven to 400°F (200°C).

Heat the olive oil in a large skillet, add the onion, chili pepper, and garlic, and fry over medium heat for 5 minutes until softened. Stir in the cumin and cook for another minute until lightly toasted.

If the beets are wet, dry out on paper towels, and then roughly chop. Add to a food processor with the onion mixture, chickpeas, breadcrumbs, and egg and blend until it all comes together but still has a little texture.

Wet your hands, then roll the mixture into 20 even-sized balls and place on a nonstick baking sheet. Sprinkle lightly with olive oil and a little sea salt and bake for 20–25 minutes until crisp and heated through.

This vivid hummus is a brilliant addition to any meal or party. Serve with charred breads and crudités for guests to tuck in to.

Beet & lemon hummus

Makes: 1 lb. 5 oz. (600 g)

3½ tablespoons (50 ml) extra virgin olive oil

1 teaspoon cumin seeds

23 oz. (660 g) canned chickpeas, drained and rinsed

4 vacuum-packed cooked beets

1 tablespoon tahini

juice of 1 lemon

salt

Add half the olive oil and half the cumin seeds along with the rest of the ingredients to a blender, season well with salt, and blend until smooth. Scoop the hummus into a serving bowl and drizzle with the remaining olive oil and cumin seeds.

15 min. / 40 hr.

Home-cured beet gravlax

Makes: 1 lb. 2 oz. (500 g)

7 oz. (200 g) raw beets, peeled

¾ cup (100 g) flaky rock salt

⅓ cup (60 g) light demerara sugar

½ cup (115 ml) vodka

1 large bunch of dill, plus extra to serve

2 lemons

3 red chili peppers, diced

3 tablespoons (50 g) jarred grated horseradish

1 × 1 lb. 8 oz. (700 g) side of salmon, skin on, scaled, and bones removed

Add the beets to a high-powered food processor along with the salt, sugar, vodka, and dill and pulse until coarse. Grate in the lemon zest, add the diced chili peppers and horseradish, and stir to combine.

Rub a little of the beet mixture onto the salmon skin, then place the salmon on a large tray, skin-side down, and pat the remaining mixture all over until the flesh is completely covered. Cover the tray tightly with plastic wrap. Pop a weight or a book on top to weigh it down and place the tray in the fridge for 40 hours.

Wearing disposable gloves, remove the salmon from the tray and brush off any excess curing mix. Pat the fillet dry with paper towels.

To serve, use a long sharp knife to slice the salmon thinly at an angle and lay out onto a platter topped with dill.

5 min. / 0 min.

Research shows that fresh beets provide powerful antioxidant, anti-inflammatory, and detoxification properties. They can act as a wonderful liver cleanser and flush out toxins.

Beet morning juice

Makes: 2 glasses

2 beets

2 carrots

1 apple

3½-inch (9 cm) piece of ginger, peeled and chopped

Using a juicer, juice all the ingredients and pour into a glass.

carrots

The carrot is a root vegetable and is a part of the Apiaceae, or Umbelliferae, family with celery, parsley, dill, and fennel. It originated in Asia, and the most common part of the plant that's eaten is the taproot; however, the stem and leaves can be eaten as well. The carrot gets its characteristic bright orange color from its high content of beta-carotene.

what's in them?

Raw carrots are 88% water, 9% carbs, 0.9% protein, 2.8% fiber, and 0.2% fat. 1 cup (130 g) raw carrot contains:

- 52 calories
- Over 10,000 mg of vitamin A, more than 4 times recommended daily intake
- Antioxidants and phytochemicals
- 410 mg potassium
- Good source of Vitamins B, C, and K

what can carrots do for me?

The high content of carotenoids in carrots gives them cancer-fighting properties. The antioxidant power of the carotenoids reduces free radicals in the body and may also regulate blood sugar. The fiber and potassium in carrots can be a protection against high blood pressure and heart disease.

how to eat carrots

Carrots are a versatile vegetable. They can be roasted, boiled, and cooked in soups and stews, giving their subtle sweet flavor. Raw, they are often eaten on their own or with a dip, and are a great addition to a juice.

varieties

The carrot is usually orange although many other colored cultivars, such as red, purple, and white, exist, which have increased in popularity.

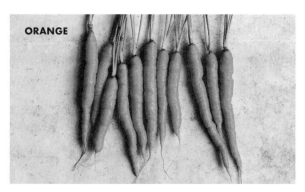

ORANGE

BABY

CHANTENAY

PURPLE

YELLOW

other varieties

Here are some less common varieties of carrot:

- **RED**: Usually sweeter than orange carrots, red carrots contain the antioxidant lycopene, which can help keep your eyes healthy

- **WHITE**: These carrots are sweeter than orange carrots and are good roasted

- **DANVERS**: An American heirloom carrot, which is orange in color and often called "half size"

- **IMPERATOR**: This variety has a deep orange color and a thin skin that is easy to peel

- **NANTES**: A French heirloom variety that is crunchy and tender with a mild taste

how to cook carrots

type of veg	quantity for 2	quantity for 4	cooking vessel	quantity of liquid	salt	oil / butter

steam

Carrot	9 oz. (250 g)		steamer	2 inches (5 cm) water in steamer	½ tablespoon	1 tablespoon butter

bake/roast

Carrot	9 oz. (250 g)		medium baking sheet		1 teaspoon	1 tablespoon olive oil

fry

Carrot	10½ oz. (300 g)		large cast-iron skillet	2 tablespoons water	1 teaspoon	1 tablespoon each vegetable oil and butter

soup

Carrot		2 lb. 10 oz. (1.2 kg)	large saucepan	2 quarts (1.8 L) vegetable broth	1 teaspoon or to taste	2 tablespoons olive oil

rice

Carrot		5-6 large carrots				

other ingredients	heat	with lid	cooking time	notes
↑ thyme leaves, freshly ground black pepper ↓	↑ medium ↓	↑ yes ↓	↑ 15 min. ↓	Peel the carrots, halve and cut them into large batons. The sweetness of the carrots pairs well with lots of flavors, such as with thyme leaves, butter, and lots of sea salt and pepper.
↑ thyme, maple syrup ↓	↑ 350°F (180°C) ↓	↑ no ↓	↑ 40–45 min. ↓	Peel and cut the carrots into 2-inch (5 cm) chunks. Toss with oil, salt and pepper, and thyme and roast for 30 minutes. Add 1 tablespoon maple syrup and roast for another 10–15 minutes.
↑ cumin seeds, honey, lemon juice ↓	↑ medium-high ↓	↑ no ↓	↑ 15 min. ↓	Use regular carrots, peeled and sliced, but baby carrots cooked whole, also work well. Heat the pan, add the oil and butter, and melt. Add the cumin and carrots in a single layer and cook for 8–10 min. Add the water, honey, and salt, and cook, stirring as needed, until tender and glazed. Finish with lemon juice to serve.
↑ 1 onion; 3 garlic cloves; ¾-inch (2 cm) piece of ginger, grated; zest and juice of 1 orange ↓	↑ medium ↓	↑ no ↓	↑ 35–45 min. ↓	Dice and sauté the vegetables and aromatics, then add broth and simmer until the carrot is very soft. For an even speedier option, grate the carrot. For a more substantial soup, add red lentils; just be sure to up the water a little if adding these.
↑ thyme ↓				Peel and chop carrots. Add to a food processor and pulse until the carrot is finely chopped and resembles rice. Use as is or add to other more substantial dishes. Consider using in a stir-fry or curry for example. Or warm through with butter and thyme and serve with a winter stew.

Spiced carrot cake

TIP

This simple spiced carrot cake is really moist so it's perfect if you need to make a cake a day or two in advance.

Makes: 8-inch (20 cm) cake
PREP / COOK TIME:
20 min. / 30 min.

1 cup (230 ml) light olive oil, plus extra for oiling
½ cup (100 g) plain yogurt
4 large eggs
1¾ cups (335 g) light muscovado sugar
2¼ cups (270 g) self-rising flour

2½ teaspoons ground cinnamon
1 teaspoon ground cardamom
1½ cups (200 g) pecans, chopped
2¾ cups (300 g) carrots, grated

8 oz. (225 g) mascarpone
¾ cup (100 g) powdered sugar
12 oz. (340 g) full-fat cream cheese
salt

01 Preheat the oven to 350°F (180°C). Oil and line the base and sides of two 8-inch (20 cm) cake pans with parchment paper. Whisk the oil, yogurt, and eggs together in a separate bowl.

02 Mix the sugar, flour, and spices with a good pinch of salt in a bowl. Add the wet ingredients to the dry, along with the carrots and half the nuts, and mix well to combine.

03 Divide the batter evenly between the pans and bake for 25–30 minutes until a skewer inserted into the center of the cake comes out clean. Let cool in the pans.

04 For the frosting, beat the mascarpone and sugar together until smooth. Add half the cream cheese and beat, then add the rest and mix until combined. Remove the cakes from the pans and sandwich together with half the frosting. Top with the remaining frosting and pecans.

PREP / COOK TIME   **TIP**   gluten-free

10 min. / 50 min.   To make this dish vegetarian, use a vegetarian Italian-
                                         style hard cheese instead of the Parmesan.

Whole roasted carrots on polenta with green sauce

Serves: 4

1 bunch of mixed carrots, leaves chopped off and half reserved

¾ cup (200 ml) olive oil

1 head garlic

2 lemons

¾ cup (200 ml) whole milk

1¼ cups (200 g) coarse polenta

2 cups (200 g) grated Parmesan cheese, plus extra to serve

¾ cup (100 g) hazelnuts, toasted

½ cup (113 g) butter

salt and pepper

Preheat the oven to 400°F (200°C).

Place the carrots on a large baking sheet with half the olive oil. Peel away all but one of the papery layers from the garlic head, then slice off the top ⅓ inch (1 cm). Place the garlic on the pan and rub it in the oil. Season well and add the zest and juice of 1 lemon. Roast for 35 minutes, tossing the carrots and garlic every 10 minutes.

Bring the milk, 3⅓ cups (800 ml) water, and 1 teaspoon salt to a boil in a large pan. Pour the polenta into the pan in a steady stream, stirring constantly for 2–3 minutes over high heat. Reduce the heat to very low and cook for 40 minutes, or until the polenta starts to come away from the pan, stirring every 5 minutes to stop it sticking.

In a blender, purée the reserved carrot tops with the remaining lemon juice, 1¼ cups (100 g) of the cheese, the nuts, and all the garlic squeezed out of their skins until smooth.

When the polenta is ready, stir in the remaining cheese and the butter. Serve the polenta with the carrots, sauce, and extra cheese.

PREP / COOK TIME

TIP

vegetarian / gluten-free / nut-free

10 min. / 1 min.

This crunchy, zesty, and spiced salad is delicious on its own or with broiled salmon for a healthy midweek lunch or dinner.

Raw ribbon salad

Serves: 4

6 mixed carrots

1 teaspoon coriander seeds

1 teaspoon nigella seeds

1 tablespoon cumin seeds

½ cup (100 g) crème fraîche or sour cream

2 tablespoons tahini

2 tablespoons apple cider vinegar

salt and pepper

3 tablespoons toasted mixed seeds, such as pumpkin, sunflower, and sesame, to garnish

Using a vegetable peeler, peel the carrots and discard the skin, then peel long thin slices of carrots onto a large platter.

In a small skillet over medium heat, toast all the spices for 1 minute, or until fragrant and toasted. Transfer to a mortar and pound them with the pestle until ground.

Mix the crème fraîche or sour cream and tahini together until smooth, then add the vinegar and mix until it is a smooth dressing. Season with salt and pepper. Drizzle the dressing over the carrots, sprinkle over the ground spices, and finish with the toasted mixed seeds.

TIP

vegetarian / gluten-free / nut-free

This is perfect if you have guests over for dinner. Pop the tray in the middle of the table and let everyone dig in. It is also great for breakfast, brunch, or lunch.

Breakfast carrot rosti tray

Serves: 4

1½ lb. (700 g) Yukon Gold potatoes, peeled and coarsely grated

4 large carrots, coarsely grated

1 tablespoon cumin seeds

1 teaspoon Dijon mustard

grated zest and juice of 1 lemon

⅔ cup (150 ml) extra virgin olive oil

4 large eggs

3¼ cups (100 g) baby spinach

1¾ oz. (50 g) feta

sea salt and pepper

Preheat the oven to 350°F (180°C).

Place the grated potatoes and carrots in a large bowl. Add a pinch of salt, then toss and scrunch it all together. Let sit for 5 minutes.

Meanwhile, mix the cumin seeds, mustard, lemon zest and juice, and 3½ tablespoons (50 ml) of the olive oil with a little pinch of salt and pepper together in a bowl. Set the dressing aside.

Place the carrot mix in a clean dish towel and squeeze out all the excess liquid, then place the mixture in a bowl. Add the remaining oil, season, and toss together. Sprinkle the mixture over a roasting pan and roast for 35 minutes, or until crispy around the edges.

Ten minutes before the rosti is ready, bring a pan of water to a boil. Reduce the heat to a simmer, then break in the eggs and poach to your liking.

Quickly toss the spinach into a dry skillet over high heat, add the dressing, and toss until wilted. Pile the spinach on the rosti, then add the poached eggs and crumble over the feta.

TIP

gluten-free / nut-free

Make extra salad and take it to work for a quick and easy lunch. For vegetarians, omit the fish sauce from the dressing, then swap the ground turkey for soy crumbles and continue with the method.

Crispy Thai-style carrot salad

Serves: 4

½ cup (115 ml) neutral oil
⅔ lb. (300 g) ground turkey
2 tablespoons grated garlic
2 tablespoons grated ginger
4 large carrots
1 cup (100 g) bean sprouts
1 bunch of Thai basil, leaves picked

Dressing
1 small red chili pepper, finely chopped
3 tablespoons fish sauce
3 tablespoons lime juice
2 teaspoons caster sugar

Pour the oil into a large skillet or wok and place over high heat. Add the ground turkey and fry, breaking it apart with a wooden spoon, for 8 minutes, or until golden and slightly crisp. Add the grated garlic and ginger and fry for another 3 minutes. Set aside.

Using a spiralizer or julienne peeler, make carrot noodles. Add to a large platter and toss in the bean sprouts and Thai basil.

Mix all the dressing ingredients together in a bowl. Toss the dressing through the carrot noodle mixture, then top with the crispy ground turkey.

This juice is a refreshing way to start the day. Celery and carrots contain vitamins A and C, which will help boost your immunity.

Carrot, celery, & ginger juice

Makes: 2 large glasses

4 carrots
1 head celery
2⅓–3½-inch (6–9 cm) piece of ginger, peeled and roughly chopped
1 handful of ice cubes, to serve

Using a juicer, juice all the ingredients and pour into 2 tall glasses. Add a couple of ice cubes and drink.

Sri Lankan carrot & coconut curry

Serves: 4

3 tablespoons ghee

2 large onions, sliced

3 cups (400 g) carrots, sliced into random diagonal 1½-inch (4 cm) chunks

2 green chili peppers, sliced lengthwise

1 large handful of curry leaves

½ teaspoon ground turmeric

1 teaspoon Sri Lankan curry powder

1 cinnamon stick

13.5 oz. (400 ml) can coconut milk

14 oz. (400 g) can chopped tomatoes

rice or roti, to serve (optional)

Heat the ghee in a saucepan over medium heat, add the onions, and fry for 10 minutes, or until soft and sticky. Add the carrots to the pan along with the chili peppers, curry leaves, and spices and fry for another 5 minutes.

Add the coconut milk and tomatoes to the pan, then reduce the heat, cover, and simmer for 25 minutes, or until the carrots are tender. Serve with rice or roti, if you like.

fermented vegetables

Fermentation is the natural process of microorganisms converting carbohydrates into alcohol or acid. In the case of vegetables, the acid is a vinegar and the vegetables become pickled. Kimchi and sauerkraut are popular fermented-vegetable mixes you can readily buy, but it is worth making your own with some of your favorite vegetables and spices.

what's in them?

The nutrient content of fermented vegetables changes depending on the vegetable/s you have used to ferment. The extra benefit from fermented vegetables is the probiotics that are contained as well as the nutrients already contained in the vegetables. Probiotics are live microorganisms, such as bacteria, yeasts, and fungi.

what can they do for me?

Fermentation is used to preserve food, but it also makes the food more digestible, it increases the micronutrients in the food, and adds beneficial microbes to the gut. Probiotics contained in fermented food have been shown to improve digestion, protect against disease, and help the immune function of the body.

how to eat fermented veg

Fermented vegetables can be eaten raw or cooked. They are a good addition to soups, salads, lunch bowls, or sandwiches. They keep unopened in jars for months. Once opened, they can be stored in the fridge for 4–6 weeks.

what you need

You don't need lots of special equipment or ingredients to start fermenting your own vegetables. Make sure all your equipment and jars are sterilized (see page 134) before you start.

CLEAN STERILIZED JAR

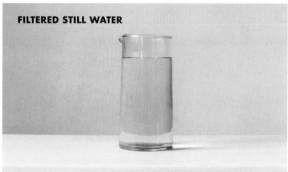

FILTERED STILL WATER

SEA SALT

SPICES / HERBS

VINEGAR

top 10 vegetables to ferment

- Carrots
- Onions
- Chili peppers
- Garlic
- Cabbage

- Beets
- Radish
- Cauliflower
- Cucumbers
- Green beans

Sterilizing your equipment

TIP

Check your jars are not damaged in any way before sterilizing. Sterilize your equipment a short time before you are ready to fill them to be sure that they remain warm for the filling process.

PREP / COOK TIME:
10 min. / 10 min.

jars with lids and / or rubber seals

funnels

spoons

01 Wash the jars, lids, funnels, and spoons in hot, soapy water.

02 If using rubber seals on jars, remove them and cover in just-boiled water. Set aside.

03 Rinse the jars, lids, funnels, and spoons thoroughly and place in a baking dish.

04 Place in a low oven for 10 minutes, or until completely dry. Set aside until ready to use.

Packing the jars

TIP

Store your pickles or fermented vegetables for at least 2 weeks before opening them. Once opened, store in the fridge for 4–6 weeks.

PREP / COOK TIME:
10 min. / 0 min.

chosen vegetables
salt
or
hot pickling liquid

spices or herbs
filtered water
(as needed)

01 If pickling, layer the prepared vegetables in the sterilized jar, leaving about 1 inch (a few centimeters) head space. If salting, mix the salt with the vegetables and the spices or herbs, then pack them tightly into the jar.

02 Pour in the hot pickling liquid, if using. When salting, if there isn't enough water, then add filtered water until the vegetables are covered.

03 Make sure the vegetables are completely covered in the liquid. Use a pestle or the end of a rolling pin to push the vegetables down into the liquid and make sure there are no air pockets.

04 Seal and let cool, then store in a cool, dark place. Softer vegetables, such as beans and cucumbers, are most likely to go soggy sooner, as they are watery.

Lemon & rosemary pickled shallots

Makes: 1 quart (1 L)

1 lb. 2 oz. (500 g) small shallots
½ cup (100 g) salt
1 lemon, zest peeled
1 bunch of rosemary
1 tablespoon fennel seeds
2 cups (500 ml) malt vinegar
⅔ cup (220 g) honey

Place the shallots in a large heatproof bowl and pour over boiling water to cover. Let cool. Once cool enough to handle, drain and peel.

Add the peeled shallots to a bowl and sprinkle with the salt. Toss well and let sit overnight.

The next day, rinse the shallots well and dry on paper towels. Place the lemon zest, juice of the lemon, rosemary, fennel seeds, vinegar, and honey in a large pan and gently heat just to dissolve the honey into the vinegar, but do not boil.

Pack the onions into a sterilized jar (see page 134) and pour over the hot vinegar mixture to fill the jar. Seal the jar and let cool. Store in a cool, dark place. The onions will be ready to eat after about 1 month. Once opened, store in the fridge for 4–6 weeks.

10 min. / 40 min.

Chili pepper sweet & sour beet pickles

Makes: 1 quart (1 L)

1½ lb. (700 g) beets, different colors and sizes

½ cup (115 ml) balsamic vinegar

1⅔ cups (400 ml) white wine vinegar

1 cup (200 g) granulated sugar or turbinado sugar

3 red chili peppers

juice of ½ lemon

1 tablespoon coriander seeds

sea salt

Place the beets in a pan of salted water and bring to a boil. Reduce the heat and simmer for 30 minutes, or until cooked, then drain and let cool. You should be able to slip off the skins once they are cool enough to handle. Halve or quarter any big ones and leave smaller ones whole.

In a separate pan, add the vinegars and sugar. Halve the chili peppers lengthwise and add to the pan along with the lemon juice, coriander seeds, and a pinch of sea salt, then bring to a boil over high heat, stirring until the sugar dissolves. Spoon the beets snugly into a sterilized jar (see page 134), then pour the pickling liquid on top. Add the chili peppers to the jar, seal, and leave for a few days before opening. Once opened, store in the fridge for 4–6 weeks.

PREP / STAND TIME

20 min. / overnight

TIP   nut-free

Check the kimchi every day, letting out some gas
and pressing the vegetables down into the brine.

Turmeric & carrot kimchi

**Makes: 6⅓ cups
(1.5 L)**

3⅓ tablespoons (50 g)
sea salt

4 tablespoons (50 g)
superfine sugar

1 napa cabbage,
quartered

1 head garlic,
cloves separated

2¾ oz. (80 g) ginger,
peeled

¾ oz. (20 g) turmeric
root

4 tablespoons (60 g)
gochugaru powder

2 tablespoons +
2 teaspoons (40 ml)
fish sauce

2 tablespoons +
2 teaspoons (40 ml)
light soy sauce

1 tablespoon Korean
shrimp paste

1 scallion, sliced

1 Korean pear, peeled
and julienned

ice

Place the salt and 2 tablespoons of the
sugar in a large bowl with 1¼ cups (300 ml)
water and stir to dissolve. Add the cabbage
with a couple of handfuls of ice cubes and
enough water to cover. Place a plate on
top to keep the cabbage weighted down
and let sit overnight.

The next day, drain the cabbage. Place the
garlic, ginger, turmeric, gochugaru powder,
fish sauce, soy sauce, shrimp paste, and
2 tablespoons sugar in a blender and
blend until smooth. Transfer the paste to a
very large bowl and add the scallion, pear,
and cabbage. Wearing disposable gloves,
massage the marinade really well into the
cabbage leaves.

Wedge the cabbage mixture into a sterilized
jar (see page 134), cover with a lid, and
let sit at room temperature for 2–5 days.
Place in the fridge for 1 month, pressing the
cabbage mix down occasionally. Store in the
fridge for up to 5 months. Once opened,
store in the fridge for 4–6 weeks.

PREP / STAND TIME

20 min. / overnight

TIP

Wash and dry the vegetables, then trim them and cut or slice into desired shapes. If the vegetables are large, halve or quarter them.

vegan / gluten-free / nut-free

Pickling vegetables

Makes: 6⅓ cups (1.5 L)

⅔ cup (130 g) coarse crystal sea salt

2¼ lb. (1 kg) radishes, carrots, pickling cucumber, pineapple, or mixed

Pickling vinegar

1 tablespoon black peppercorns

1 tablespoon coriander seeds

1 tablespoon yellow mustard seeds

few pieces of mace blades

2 bay leaves

3 cups (700 ml) white wine vinegar

¾ cup (150 g) turbinado sugar

2-inch (5 cm) piece of ginger, peeled and thinly sliced

In a large bowl, mix the coarse sea salt with 1¼ cups (300 ml) boiling water and let it dissolve to make a brining solution. Add 5 cups (1.2 L) cold water, then the vegetables. Cover and let soak overnight.

The next day, rinse and drain the soaked vegetables. To make the pickling vinegar, put the whole spices in a dry saucepan and toast over low heat until they begin to smell aromatic. Add the bay leaves, then add the vinegar and sugar and warm gently until the sugar dissolves. Bring to a simmer and add the ginger.

Pack the vegetables into a sterilized jar (see page 134), pour over the hot vinegar, then seal. Leave in a cool, dark place for at least 2 weeks. Once opened, store in the fridge for 4–6 weeks.

15 min. / 10 min.

Pickling chili peppers

Makes: 1 quart (1 L)

1 lb. 2 oz. (500 g) mixed red and green chili peppers

15 black peppercorns

2 tablespoons coriander seeds

1 tablespoon allspice berries

6 heaped tablespoons caster sugar

3½ cups (850 ml) white wine vinegar

5 teaspoons flaky sea salt

5 bay leaves

Prick the chili peppers with a sharp knife, then place in a large bowl and pour over enough boiling water to cover. Let sit for 5 minutes, then drain and pat dry with paper towels.

Add all the spices to a dry saucepan and lightly toast for 1 minute over medium heat. Add the sugar, then pour in the vinegar and warm gently until the sugar dissolves.

Pack the chili peppers into a sterilized canning jar (see page 134). Add the salt and bay leaves and pour in the vinegar mixture. The liquid needs to cover the chili peppers. Let cool, then seal and leave in the fridge for at least 2 weeks before opening. Once opened, store in the fridge for 4–6 weeks.

TIP

Make sure all your equipment is sterilized (page 134). Keep the sauerkraut at an even, cool temperature—too cool and it will take longer, but too warm and the sauerkraut may become moldy.

Sauerkraut

Makes: 6⅓ cups (1.5 L) jar

4½ lb. (2 kg) green cabbage, any leathery outer leaves removed, cored and thinly shredded

6 tablespoons flaky sea salt

1 tablespoon caraway seeds

2 teaspoons black peppercorns

grated zest and juice of 1 lemon

Layer the cabbage and salt in a clean bowl, then massage the salt into the cabbage for 5 minutes. Wait 5 minutes, then repeat. You should end up with a much-reduced volume of cabbage sitting in its own brine. Mix in the caraway seeds, peppercorns, and lemon zest and juice.

Cover the surface of the cabbage with plastic wrap, then press out all the air bubbles from below. Weigh the cabbage down with a couple of heavy plates, making sure as much of the cabbage as possible is covered. The brine will rise to cover the cabbage a little. Cover the bowl with plastic wrap and leave in a cool, dark place for at least 5 days. Check the cabbage every day or so, releasing any gases and stirring the cabbage to release the bubbles. If any scum forms, remove it, then rinse the weights in boiling water and replace the plastic wrap. You should see bubbles appearing within the cabbage. It will be ready to eat after 5 days, but for maximum flavor, let the cabbage ferment for 2–6 weeks, or until the bubbling subsides. When you like the flavor, transfer it to smaller sterilized jars, and store in the fridge for up to 6 months. Once opened, store in the fridge for 4–6 weeks.

tomatoes

Tomatoes are technically a fruit but more often treated
as a vegetable. They are the red berry of the tomato plant.

what's in them?

Tomatoes have a very high water content, no cholesterol, and
for such a sweet vegetable, only a small amount of carbohydrates
per serving. 1 cup (180 g) chopped raw tomato contains:

- 32 calories
- 427 mg potassium
- 25 mg vitamin C
- The powerful antioxidant lycopene as well as lutein and zeaxanthin

- 1.6 g protein
- 2.2 g fiber
- 100% daily recommended intake for vitamin A
- 5.8 g carbohydrates

what can they do for me?

The powerful antioxidants in tomatoes have been found to
contribute to a number of health benefits. Lycopene is thought to
play a role in cancer prevention while lutein and zeaxanthin may
protect vision. A study showed daily intake of these antioxidants
had a 25% reduction of age-related macular degeneration.

how to eat tomatoes

Tomatoes are a source of the fifth taste: umami. They can be
eaten in many ways and in a variety of dishes. Cooking tomatoes
releases more of the powerful antioxidant lycopene. It is also
important to wash tomatoes before eating or buy organic as they
are known to hold high levels of pesticide residue.

varieties:

Here are the most popular and well-known varieties:

ROMA

POINTED PLUM

RED BEEFSTEAK TOMATO

YELLOW HEIRLOOM

GREEN ZEBRA

BLACK HEIRLOOM

YELLOW CHERRY

RED CHERRY

how to cook tomatoes

type of veg	quantity for 2	quantity for 4	cooking vessel	quantity of liquid	salt	oil / butter

bake/roast

Tomatoes	9 oz. (250 g)		medium baking pan		1 teaspoon	1 tablespoon olive oil

fry

Tomatoes	1 lb. 2 oz. (500 g) tomatoes, chopped		large high-sided sauté pan or skillet		1 teaspoon	1 tablespoon olive oil

soup

Tomatoes		2 lb. 10 oz. (1.2 kg) ripe tomatoes	large saucepan	5 cups (1.2 L) vegetable broth	to taste	1 tablespoon olive oil

confit

Tomatoes		4½ lb. (2 kg) tomatoes	high-sided roasting pan		2 teaspoons	2 cups (500 ml) extra virgin olive oil

other ingredients	heat	with lid	cooking time	notes
	↑ 400°F (200°C) ↓	↑ no ↓	↑ 30 min. ↓	Roasted cherry tomatoes on the vine make a perfect side, or they can be smashed up and used in a pasta sauce. The tomato skins will burst and the skin will take on a lovely slight char.
1 small onion, chopped; 1 garlic clove, chopped; 1 tablespoon tomato paste or 3 sundried tomatoes; chopped, 1 teaspoon dried oregano	↑ medium ↓	↑ no ↓	↑ 30 min. ↓	Sweat the onion and garlic in the oil over low heat for 10 min. until soft and sweet. Add the chopped tomatoes, tomato paste or sundried tomatoes, herbs, and a little seasoning and cook until reduced. The sauce can be used as is or puréed. It makes a great base for pizza, pasta sauces, or stews.
1 onion, 1 small carrot, 1 celery stalk, 2 teaspoons tomato paste, pinch of sugar, ground black pepper	↑ medium-high ↓	↑ no ↓	↑ 30 min. ↓	Dice the onion, carrot, and celery and sauté in the oil for 5-10 min. Add the tomato paste and chopped tomatoes with the remaining ingredients and bring to a boil, then simmer until the vegetables are soft. Blend using a handheld blender.
↑ 2 heads garlic, 1 teaspoon mustard seeds, 1 teaspoon coriander seeds ↓	↑ 300°F (150°C) ↓	↑ no ↓	↑ 2 hr. ↓	Place your whole tomatoes into the roasting pan; the more snugly they fit, the better. Scatter over the garlic cloves, slightly bashed, followed by the spices and salt. Roast until sticky and slightly reduced.

Perfect confit tomatoes

TIP

vegetarian / gluten-free / nut-free

Use a baking dish that will fit all the tomatoes snugly. If it's too big it will affect the amount of oil you will need. These are great served with Greek yogurt.

Makes: 5 cups (1.2 L)
PREP / COOK TIME: 10 min. / 2 hr.

- 4½ lb. (2 kg) mixed tomatoes
- 2 heads garlic, bashed, with skin left on
- 1 teaspoon mustard seeds, ground
- 1 teaspoon coriander seeds, ground
- 2 teaspoons salt
- 2 cups (500 ml) extra virgin olive oil

01 Preheat the oven to 300°F (150°C). Put the tomatoes into a large baking dish and add the garlic cloves, ground spices, and salt.

02 Pour in the olive oil, making sure it comes two-thirds of the way up the tomatoes. Roast for 2 hours, or until sticky and reduced slightly.

03 Let the tomatoes cool a little, then squeeze out the garlic from its papery skins and add to the tomatoes.

04 Pack the tomatoes and oil into sterilized jars (see page 134) and seal. Store in a cool place. Once opened, store in the fridge for up to 2 weeks.

PREP / COOK TIME

TIP

vegan / nut-free

10 min. / 0 min.

Be sure to use ripe tomatoes for maximum flavor.
Make extra soup and freeze in an ice-cube tray.
This soup can also be served hot on a cold day.

Tomato gazpacho

Serves: 4

1¾ lb. (800 g) ripe
tomatoes, halved
½ cucumber, peeled and
roughly chopped, plus
a handful of diced
pieces, to serve
2 jarred red peppers
2 garlic cloves
2 oz. (60 g) sourdough
bread, roughly torn
1 tablespoon sherry
vinegar
3½ tablespoons (50 ml)
extra virgin olive oil, plus
extra for drizzling
1 handful of basil leaves
salt and pepper

Purée the tomatoes, cucumber, peppers, garlic, bread, vinegar, and olive oil with salt and pepper in a blender or food processor until combined.

Push through a fine-mesh sieve into a bowl, cover with plastic wrap, and chill for a few hours. You can also make this well in advance.

Serve the soup in bowls, topped with the basil leaves, diced cucumber, and an extra drizzle of olive oil. Drop a couple of ice cubes into the bowls before serving if you like the soup very cold.

15 min. / 50 min.

Serve this curry with cooked basmati rice,
rotis, or flatbreads for a special dinner.

Tomato & lemon curry

Serves: 4

3 tablespoons ghee

2 onions, roughly sliced

8 garlic cloves,
finely sliced

1 lemon, finely chopped,
seeds removed

1 teaspoon ground
turmeric

20 fresh curry leaves

1 tablespoon Sri Lankan
curry powder

13.5 oz. (400 ml) can
coconut milk

15 tomatoes,
roughly chopped

½ cup (50 g) coconut
flakes

salt

Heat the ghee in a saucepan over medium heat, add the onions, and fry for 10–15 minutes until soft and sweet. Add the garlic, chopped lemon flesh, and turmeric and cook for another few minutes until the garlic starts to soften a little.

Add the curry leaves and cook until fragrant, then add the curry powder and stir for a minute to toast a little. Add the coconut milk and tomatoes and cook for 30 minutes, stirring occasionally.

Meanwhile, toast the coconut flakes in a dry skillet until golden.

Taste the curry and season with salt, then ladle into bowls and top with the toasted coconut.

15 min. / 15 min.

This dish is excellent when tomatoes are in season and at their best. For a vegetarian version, omit the anchovies.

Panzanella

**Serves: 2–4
as a side**

7 oz. (200 g) sourdough bread
½ cup (115 ml) olive oil
2 garlic cloves, grated
1 lb. 5 oz. (600 g) ripe mixed tomatoes, roughly chopped
1 small red onion, very finely sliced
8 anchovy fillets in oil, drained and roughly chopped
2 tablespoons red wine vinegar
1 bunch of basil, leaves picked
salt and pepper

Preheat the oven to 350°F (180°C).

Tear the bread into 1¼-inch (3 cm) pieces and place on a large baking pan. Add half the olive oil and the grated garlic and toss well. Season with salt and pepper and bake for 15 minutes, tossing every few minutes, or until golden and crispy.

Place the tomatoes in a large bowl and season with salt and pepper. Add the onion, toasted bread, and anchovies. Toss the mixture together with your hands, then stir in the vinegar and remaining olive oil. Taste and add a little more salt, pepper, vinegar, or oil, if needed. Tear in the basil leaves, toss together, and serve.

10 min. / 12 min.

One-pan tomato spaghetti

Serves: 4

14 oz. (400 g) spaghetti
1 lb. 5 oz. (600 g)
mixed cherry tomatoes,
chopped
4 garlic cloves,
finely sliced
1 red chili pepper,
finely sliced
⅔ cup (150 ml) extra
virgin olive oil
grated zest and juice
of 1 lemon
1 handful of basil leaves
4 cups (1 L) hot vegetable
broth
salt and pepper
grated Parmesan cheese,
to serve

In a large shallow pan with a lid, add the pasta, tomatoes, garlic, chili pepper, olive oil, lemon zest and juice, 2 heaped teaspoons salt, half the basil leaves, and the hot broth. Bring to a boil over high heat and cover with a lid. Cook for 9 minutes, or until the pasta is al dente and the liquid has nearly evaporated, but leaving behind a healthy amount of sauce, stirring and turning the pasta frequently with tongs.

Season to taste, then divide among 4 bowls. Sprinkle over the reserved basil and serve with grated Parmesan.

onions & garlic

Garlic is considered a vegetable and is a part of the allium family along with onions, shallots, leeks, and chives. Garlic and onions can be distinguished by the bulb size, their nutrition, and flavor.

what's in onions?

- 64 calories in 1 cup (160 g)
- Vitamin C
- Vitamin B6
- Manganese
- Sulfur compounds

what's in garlic?

- Vitamin C
- Vitamin B6
- Manganese
- Sulfur compounds

what can onions do for me?

As with garlic and other allium vegetables, the sulfur compounds onions are known to help protect against cancer. The high vitamin C builds and maintains collagen, which can boost skin and hair.

what can garlic do for me?

Garlic is a natural antibiotic and has been used in cooking and medicine for a long time. It contains a compound called diallyl sulfide, which is said to be more effective in fighting bacteria than some antibiotics.

how to eat onions

Onions are used in many different dishes. When sautéed, the heat is cooked out of them and they bring a sweetness and flavor to the dish. Onions can also be eaten raw.

how to eat garlic

Cooking garlic reduces its flavor but also its health benefits. Finely chopped, it can be eaten raw in dressings and dips. The greens can also be eaten in stir-fries or salads.

onion varieties

Onions can vary in size, shape, color, and also flavor. The most common types include:

other varieties

- **VIDALIA:** A variety of sweet onion grown in the US

WHITE

SHALLOT

PEARL

SPANISH BROWN ONION

LEEK

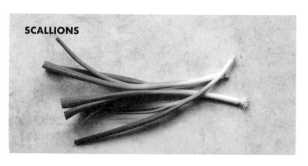

SCALLIONS

garlic varieties:

There are many types of garlic, each with different flavors:

- **ELEPHANT:** A variant of leek, this huge allium is sweeter and milder than traditional garlic

- **RAMSON:** This is wild garlic and is found in moist woodland; pick in April and May

RED

GREEN GARLIC

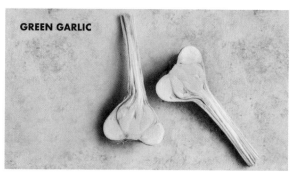

how to cook onions

type of veg	quantity for 2	quantity for 4	cooking vessel	quantity of liquid	salt	oil / butter

bake/roast

type of veg	quantity for 2	quantity for 4	cooking vessel	quantity of liquid	salt	oil / butter
Onions	2 large onions, approx. 1 lb. (450 g)		↑			↑
			small baking dish			1 tablespoon olive oil
Garlic	1 head		↓			↓

fry

type of veg	quantity for 2	quantity for 4	cooking vessel	quantity of liquid	salt	oil / butter
Onions	2 large onions, approx. 1 lb. (450 g)		large heavy saucepan	4–5 tablespoons water or as needed	1 teaspoon	1 tablespoon unsalted butter
Garlic	6 cloves		small skillet			4 tablespoons (60 ml) olive oil

slow cook

type of veg	quantity for 2	quantity for 4	cooking vessel	quantity of liquid	salt	oil / butter
Onions		4 large onions (white, yellow, brown, or red)	large high-sided skillet	5–6 tablespoons broth or water, or as needed	¼ teaspoon	2 tablespoons unsalted butter
Garlic		3 heads garlic, cloves separated	small heavy saucepan			1–1½ cups (250–350 ml) olive oil or duck fat

& garlic

other ingredients	heat	with lid	cooking time	notes
	↑ 350°F (180°C) ↓	↑ no ↓	45–50 min. 30–45 min.	Slice the rooted end off the onions, but leave them in their skins. Roast until tender, sticky, and caramelized. Either cook as a whole head or remove the cloves from the garlic but keep them in their skins. Once they are sticky and soft they are amazing squeezed out onto bread or stirred into salad dressings and sauces.
	low medium-low	↑ no ↓	35–50 min. 3–5 min.	Halve and peel the onions. Cut lengthwise into even, thin slices, ¼ inch (5 mm) thick. Melt the butter in a pan, add the onions and salt, and fry for several minutes, stirring. Reduce the heat to low and cook, stirring occasionally, until soft, sticky, and golden. As the onions gain color, you may need to add a little water to the pan to prevent sticking/burning. Peel and thinly slice the garlic cloves. Gently heat the oil, add the garlic, and cook, stirring until the garlic is light golden. Remove from the heat and strain using a fine-mesh sieve, retaining the garlic oil. Drain and cool the garlic slices on paper towels. As they cool they will become crisp. The infused oil can be used to cook with or use added to a dressing.
2 teaspoons brown sugar, ¼ teaspoon ground black pepper, 1 thyme sprig, 2 teaspoons balsamic vinegar	medium-low	yes	↑	Halve and peel the onions. Cut lengthwise into even, thin slices, ¼ inch (5 mm) thick. Melt the butter in a pan, add the onions and salt and stir to combine. Cover the onions with a wet piece of parchment paper, reduce the heat to low, and cover with a lid. Cook for 15–20 min. until soft and sweet. Once softened, remove the lid and paper, stir in the additional ingredients, and cook, stirring, until deep golden and sticky.
2 bay leaves, 3 teaspoons whole black or pink peppercorns	low	no	45–60 min. ↓	Separate the garlic cloves and remove any papery skins. Crush lightly, place in a small pan with the bay and peppercorns. Cover with oil and heat gently until the oil reaches 121°F (100°C). Simmer for 10 min., reduce the heat to very low, and cook for another 30 min.

20 min. / 55 min.

Onion tart

Serves: 4

5 tablespoons ghee
1 lb. 14 oz. (850 g) large onions, finely sliced
11½ oz. (320 g) puff pastry
1 egg, beaten
2 tablespoons Dijon mustard
2 tablespoons baby capers
¾ cup (100 g) frozen peas
½ teaspoon thyme leaves
3½ oz. (100 g) Lancashire cheese

Preheat the oven 350°F (180°C).

Heat the ghee in a large saucepan over medium heat, add the onions, and cook for 5 minutes. Reduce the heat, cover, and let cook for 30 minutes, stirring the onions every 5 minutes. Uncover, increase the heat, and cook, stirring frequently, until the onions brown and caramelize.

Place the pastry on a large nonstick baking sheet. Using a sharp knife, score a ¾-inch (2 cm) border around the edge of the pastry, making sure not to cut all the way through. Glaze the edge of the pastry with the beaten egg. Spread the mustard over the base of the tart and pile on the onions, spreading them out evenly. Sprinkle over the capers, peas, and thyme, then break over chunks of the cheese.

Bake for 20 minutes, or until the pastry is golden brown.

30 min. / 1–1½ hr.

Confit garlic

Makes: 18 ounces (500 g)

6 heads garlic, peeled

2 shallots, quartered

3 bay leaves

4 thyme sprigs

1 red chili pepper, stabbed with a knife

1¼ cups (285 ml) olive oil

salt

Preheat the oven to 300°F (150°C).

Place the garlic, shallots, bay leaves, thyme, and chili pepper in an oven-safe dish. Sprinkle in 1 teaspoon salt, then pour in the olive oil. It should cover the garlic and shallots.

Place the dish in the oven and cook for 1–1½ hours until the garlic is sticky and soft.

Remove from the oven and pour into a sterilized jar (see page 134). Seal and store in the fridge for 1–2 weeks. Always use a clean spoon to scoop the garlic out.

20 min. / 40 min.

To make this risotto dairy-free, use olive oil,
a vegan cheese, and a good-quality vegetable broth.

Onion & garlic risotto

Serves: 4

4½ cups (1.1 L) chicken broth

4 tablespoons (60 ml) olive oil

10 garlic cloves, finely sliced

2 large onions, finely diced

½ head celery, finely diced

2 cups (400 g) arborio rice

2 cups (500 ml) dry white wine

½ cup (113 g) unsalted butter

1½ cups (150 g) grated Parmesan cheese, plus extra to serve

salt and pepper

Pour the broth into a saucepan and heat over medium heat.

Pour the olive oil into a heavy saucepan, add the garlic, and fry for 3 minutes, or until golden and crisp. Scoop out the garlic and set aside on a plate. Add the onions and celery to the pan and fry gently for about 15 minutes, or until softened but not colored.

Add the rice and increase the heat. After 1 minute the rice will start to look slightly translucent. Add the wine and keep stirring for a few more minutes until it has evaporated. Start adding the hot broth, a ladleful at a time, until each addition of broth has almost been absorbed into the rice. Continue doing this while stirring constantly. Carry on adding broth until the rice is soft but still with a slight bite. It should take about 15 minutes.

Remove the pan from the heat, add the butter and Parmesan, and season with salt and pepper. Cover and let stand for 2 minutes. Sprinkle over the crispy garlic and extra Parmesan.

20 min. / 50 min.

Whole sticky roasted Persian-style onions

Serves: 4

8 white onions
3 bay leaves
4 garlic cloves
2 x 14 oz. (400 g) cans tomatoes
1 teaspoon ground cinnamon
1 tablespoon Persian mixed spice (advieh)
1½ cups (300 g) basmati rice
1 cup (226 g) butter, cut into cubes
1 handful of mint, parsley, and dill leaves
salt and pepper

Preheat the oven to 375°F (190°C).

Slice the bottoms off the onions and place them in a bowl. Pour boiling water over the onions to cover and let stand for 10 minutes.

Meanwhile, add all the remaining ingredients, except the herbs, to a deep baking dish, roughly 12 × 8 inches (30 × 20 cm). Add 1 cup (230 ml) boiling water and season well with salt and pepper.

Drain the onions and slide off the skins. Dot the onions into the mix, pushing them in so they are half-submerged. Cover with foil and bake for 30 minutes.

Remove and stir the sauce gently. Return to the oven without the foil for another 20 minutes. Sprinkle over the herbs and serve.

Garlic & almond soup

TIP   nut-free

If you have made the confit garlic on page 168, simply ignore the roasted garlic step in this recipe and use the confit garlic instead—it will taste even better.

Serves: 4–6

PREP / COOK TIME:
15 min. / 40 min.

4 large heads garlic, bashed and skins still on
3½ tablespoons (50 ml) extra virgin olive oil
2 onions, finely chopped

1 cup (200 g) crème fraîche or sour cream
4 cups (1 L) chicken broth
10½ oz. (300 g) ciabatta, roughly torn

2 tablespoons sherry vinegar
⅔ cup (100 g) whole blanched almonds, lightly toasted
salt and pepper

01 Preheat the oven to 350°F (180°C). Add the garlic to a small roasting dish and drizzle over half the olive oil. Roast for 25 minutes, tossing halfway through.

02 Meanwhile, heat the remaining olive oil in a heavy pan over medium heat, add the onions, and slowly fry for 10 minutes, or until really soft and translucent. Remove from the heat and set aside.

03 Once the garlic is ready, remove from the oven and cool slightly before squeezing them out of their skins. Add to the onions along with the crème fraîche or sour cream and broth.

04 Add the ciabatta and vinegar to the pan, then simmer for 5 minutes. Add the toasted almonds. Remove from the heat and, using a handheld blender, blend until smooth. Ladle into bowls, drizzle with olive oil, and add lots of pepper.

20 min. / 1 hr. 10 min.

40 clove roast garlic chicken

Serves: 4

4 heads garlic
or 40 cloves
¼ cup (57 g) butter
4½ lb. (2 kg) whole
chicken
2 cups (500 ml)
white wine
2¼ lb. (1 kg) new
potatoes
1 bunch of tarragon
2 cups (300 g) peas
1 cup (200 g) crème
fraîche or sour cream
juice of 1 lemon
salt and cracked black
pepper

Preheat the oven to 350°F (180°C).

Bash the garlic open so the skins are still attached to the cloves but all the cloves have separated.

Rub the butter over the skin of the chicken and season really well with salt and pepper.

Sprinkle half the garlic in the middle of a high-sided roasting pan. Place the remaining garlic inside the cavity of the chicken and place the chicken on the garlic in the pan. Pour in the wine, add the potatoes and tarragon, and roast the chicken, brushing occasionally with the pan juices, for about 1 hour 10 minutes, or until cooked through.

Remove the chicken from the pan and let rest on a board. Place the pan over medium heat, add the peas and stir in the crème fraîche or sour cream. Add the lemon juice and taste and adjust the seasoning. Either place the chicken in the middle of the pan and serve family-style or carve and serve with greens.

Onion & garlic bhajis

vegetarian / gluten-free / nut-free

TIP

These crispy, light, spiced bhajis are perfect for a dinner party or drinks with friends. Serve with a dipping sauce or a mango chutney.

Makes: 18 bhajis

PREP / COOK TIME:
10 min. / 15 min.

3 onions, finely sliced
5 garlic cloves, sliced
½ teaspoon baking powder

1¾ cups (200 g) chickpea flour
½ teaspoon chili powder
½ teaspoon ground turmeric

30 curry leaves
1 green chili pepper, chopped
vegetable oil, for frying
salt

01 Soak the onion and garlic slices in a large bowl of cold water.

02 Sift the baking powder and flour into a bowl, then add the spices, curry leaves, chopped chili pepper, and 1 teaspoon salt. Pour in about ½ cup (115 ml) cold water to make a thick batter.

03 Drain the onion and garlic and mix into the batter. Heat 2 inches (5 cm) of oil in a wok or deep pan. Add a tiny speck of batter. If it rises to the surface surrounded by bubbles and starts to brown, then the oil is hot enough for frying.

04 Lower a few heaped tablespoons of the bhaji mixture at a time into the pan and fry for 3–4 minutes, turning once, until they are evenly browned and crisp. Drain on paper towels. Sprinkle with salt. Keep warm while you cook the rest.

sprouts

Sprouting is the process that occurs naturally by which seeds germinate and put out shoots. There are a variety of seeds that can be sprouted for eating, all of which have excellent nutritional value. The process of sprouting legumes and cereals has also become very popular as it converts the seed to a more digestible food.

what's in them?

Sprouts are rich in digestible energy, proteins, and plant compounds, which are needed in higher amounts to allow the germinating plant to grow, hence their high nutritional value. Each sprouted seed differs slightly in its nutritional makeup. The alfalfa sprout is one of the more common. 1 cup (35 g) alfalfa sprouts contains:

- 8 calories
- 30.5 mg vitamins K and C
- A variety of plant compounds including saponins, flavonoids, and phytoestrogens
- Minerals including phosphorus, zinc, iron, and magnesium

what can they do for me?

The sprouting process naturally begins to break down the contained complex compounds found in legumes, which are often known as "pre-digested foods." The content of vitamins, fatty acids, proteins, and fibers increases as the sprouting process occurs. Studies have shown the increased antioxidants help to reduce inflammation, and sprouts have been used to treat a range of conditions such as arthritis and kidney issues.

how to eat sprouts

Sprouts are generally enjoyed raw in salads and sandwiches or as a garnish on a meal.

varieties

There is an endless list of legumes and seeds that can be germinated into sprouts. Here are some of the most well-known:

ALFALFA

CHICKPEA SPROUTS

MUNG BEANS

SPROUTED PEAS

BEAN SPROUTS

CRESS SPROUTS

other varieties

- **BROCCOLI SPROUTS**: very young broccoli plants, which look like alfalfa sprouts
- **FENUGREEK SPROUTS**: Long, slender plants with a mild curry flavor
- **RADISH SPROUTS**: With a mild peppery flavor, these are sprouted from red radish or mooli (daikon) seeds
- **WHEATGRASS**: Sprouted from the common wheat plant in just 2 days

How to sprout

TIP

Use a wide-neck jar and muslin cloth to sprout your seeds or use a ready-made sprouting jar or tray. If they start to go moldy, discard, and start again.

Makes: 1¾ oz. (50 g)

PREP / COOK TIME:
5 min. / 0 min.

2 tablespoons seeds, nuts, grains, or pulses suitable for home sprouting

01 Rinse the seeds thoroughly in cold water.

02 If using a jar, place them in a large clean glass jar, about one-third full, and fill the jar about three-quarters full with lukewarm water. Seal and leave to soak overnight.

03 The next day, rinse and drain thoroughly, then cover the jar with muslin. Secure the muslin to the top of the jar with a rubber band. Place the jar upside down. If using a tray, be sure there is no water in the bottom.

04 Rinse and drain daily for 2–5 days until sprouts start to appear. Once the seeds have fully sprouted, rinse them well and store in the fridge. Use within 2–3 days.

how to sprout

Soaking time	Rinse & drain	Sprouting time	Harvest	Notes

sunflower

| 8–12 hr. | Every 8 hr. | 1–3 days | When little shoots appear | Use hulled or unhulled seeds for sprouting. Toasted seeds will not sprout. Add to salads, sandwiches, and wraps, also good added to smoothies. |

pumpkin (hulled)

| 8 hr. | Every 8 hr. | 3 days | When little shoots appear | These are quite difficult to sprout so soak in warm water overnight. Add sprouts to salad, sandwiches, and wraps. |

hemp

| 4–12 hr. | 2 times/day | 3–6 days | When leaves open | The flavor is similar to sunflower sprouts. Add to salads, sandwiches, and wraps. |

cress

| 4–12 hr. | Every 12 hr. | Up to 5 days | When leaves open | Ideal for adding to sandwiches, wraps, or salads. Use as a garnish on soups. |

mustard

| 6–12 hr. | 2–3 times/ day | Up to 6 days | When most of leaves open | Their flavor is quite spicy. Good mixed into a salad. |

radish

| 6–12 hr. | 2–3 times/day | Up to 6 days | When leaves open | These have a spicy punch. Great added to a salad or as a garnish to soups. |

broccoli

| 6–12 hr. | 2–3 times/day | Up to 6 days | When leaves open | These have a spicy punch. Great added to a salad or as a garnish to soups. |

Soaking time	Rinse & drain	Sprouting time	Harvest	Notes

fenugreek

Soaking time	Rinse & drain	Sprouting time	Harvest	Notes
6–12 hr.	2–3 times/ day	Up to 6 days	When leaves open	Add to soups or salads.

kale

Soaking time	Rinse & drain	Sprouting time	Harvest	Notes
6–12 hr.	2–3 times/day	Up to 6 days	When leaves open	Toss into a salad, add to a sandwich, or use as a garnish.

chickpeas

Soaking time	Rinse & drain	Sprouting time	Harvest	Notes
24 hr.	2–3 times/day	Up to 4 days	When little tails appear	Make into a nutritious hummus, add to salads, or use as a garnish to meals.

alfalfa

Soaking time	Rinse & drain	Sprouting time	Harvest	Notes
8–12 hr.	2–3 times/day	Up to 6 days	When leaves open	Add to a salad for an extra crunch, or use in a sandwich, or add to a stir-fry.

red clover

Soaking time	Rinse & drain	Sprouting time	Harvest	Notes
8–12 hr.	2–3 times/day	Up to 6 days	When leaves open	These look similar to alfalfa but have a milder flavor. Great in salads or use as a garnish.

mung beans

Soaking time	Rinse & drain	Sprouting time	Harvest	Notes
8–12 hr.	2–3 times/day	Up to 5 days	When most have short roots	Add to stir-fries or salads.

lentils

Soaking time	Rinse & drain	Sprouting time	Harvest	Notes
7 hr.	2–3 times/day	Up to 3 days	When most have short roots	Add to stir-fries or salads.

TIP

Use vegetables that are in season for this bowl. For a protein-packed dinner, serve with crispy roasted chicken thighs or tofu steaks.

Hummus, quinoa, and beet bowl

Serves: 2

juice of ½ lemon
1 green chili pepper, chopped
5 oz. (150 g) store-bought hummus
2 different-colored beets
½ cup (100 g) cooked quinoa
1 cup (100 g) pea sprouts
1 large handful of basil and mint leaves
½ cup (50 g) toasted mixed seeds, such as pumpkin, sunflower, and sesame

Stir the lemon juice and chopped chili pepper into the hummus, then divide the hummus equally between 2 bowls and spoon it around so it roughly covers the base of the bowls.

Using a mandoline or a sharp knife, finely slice the beets, keeping them in their own piles.

Pile the quinoa into the bowls, top with a pile of sprouts, beets, herbs, and finish with a flurry of toasted mixed seeds.

10 min. / 5 min.

Alfalfa & charred corn salad

Serves: 4

3 corn cobs,
husked and kernels
removed from cobs
1 small shallot,
cut into rings
4 tablespoons (60 ml)
olive oil
1 red chili pepper, sliced
2 limes
1 cup (225 g) skyr or
Greek yogurt
½ cup (50 g) grated
Parmesan cheese
4½ cups (150 g) alfalfa
sprouts
salt and pepper

Place a large heavy pan over high heat and once hot, add the corn kernels and toss around until charred and starting to pop a little.

Mix the shallot, olive oil, sliced chili pepper, and juice and zest of 1 lime together in a bowl. Season well with salt and pepper and set aside.

Mix the yogurt and most of the Parmesan together and season well with salt and pepper. Add the juice and zest of the remaining lime and spoon the mixture onto plates. Top with the corn and finish with a big mountain of sprouts and the remaining Parmesan.

10 min. / 15 min.

Crispy alfalfa & kale salad

Serves: 4

½ cup (115 ml) olive oil
1 tablespoon cumin seeds
1 tablespoon apple cider vinegar
1 large bunch purple kale
3 cups (100 g) alfalfa sprouts
1 lb. 8oz. (660 g) canned chickpeas, drained
2 tablespoons rose harissa paste
seeds of 1 pomegranate
salt and pepper

Preheat the oven to 425°F (220°C).

Place the olive oil, cumin seeds, vinegar, and a good pinch of salt and pepper together in a large bowl and whisk until combined.

Tear the kale leaves away from the stems into bite-sized pieces. Toss through the oil mixture, then sprinkle over 2 large baking sheets. Bake for 5 minutes. Remove and mix through the sprouts, tossing everything well, then return to the oven for another 5–10 minutes until crisp.

Place the chickpeas in a bowl and mix in the harissa paste and pomegranate seeds. Season to taste.

Toss the kale and chickpeas together and serve.

PREP / COOK TIME

20 min. / 0 min.

TIP

vegan / gluten-free

For a perfect vegan dinner, bulk this salad up
with a little crispy eggplant and tofu for protein.
Or for fish-eaters, serve with broiled giant prawns.

Crunchy Thai cashew & mixed sprout salad

Serves: 2

4 mixed-color carrots
1 mango, peeled and
thinly sliced
1 bunch of cilantro and
mint, leaves picked
2–3 cups (150 g) mixed
sprouts or chickpea
sprouts
⅔ cup (100 g) cashews,
toasted and chopped

Dressing

2 tablespoons lime juice
1 tablespoon soy sauce
1 teaspoon toasted
sesame oil
1 red chili pepper, diced
2-inch (5 cm) piece of
ginger, peeled and
grated

Mix all the dressing ingredients together in a small bowl and
set aside.

If you have a spiralizer, spiralize the carrots into noodles or
use a vegetable peeler. Place in a bowl, add all the remaining
ingredients, and toss together until combined. Place on a large
platter and drizzle over the dressing and serve.

15 min. / 0 min.

Crispy mung bean sprout salad

Serves: 4

grated zest and juice of 1 lemon

1 tablespoon tamarind chutney

1 teaspoon toasted cumin seeds

1 large bunch of cilantro, leaves picked

½ cup (112 g) plain yogurt

2 large tomatoes, diced

1 medium cucumber, diced

1 red onion, finely diced

1 cup (100 g) sprouted mung beans

7 oz. (200 g) bhel puri snack mix or papadums, roughly crushed

salt and pepper

Mix the lemon zest and juice, the tamarind chutney, and cumin seeds together in a bowl to combine. Season to taste.

Add half the cilantro and the yogurt with a good pinch of salt to a blender and blend until smooth and vivid green.

Toss the chopped tomatoes, cucumber, red onion, and sprouted mung beans together in a large bowl, then fold through the tamarind dressing. Sprinkle over the bhel puri mix and drizzle with the yogurt sauce. Garnish with the remaining cilantro leaves.

peppers

The bell pepper or sweet pepper is another type of botanical fruit that is used in the culinary world as a vegetable. They belong to the nightshade family and are related to chili peppers, but they are lacking in the chemical "capsaicin," which leaves them sweet instead of hot.

what's in them?

Peppers are made up of 94% water, 6% carbs (mostly sugars), and near to no fat or protein. 1 cup (150 g) chopped raw red pepper contains:

- 39 calories
- More than double the daily requirement of vitamin C (190 mg)
- Vitamin B6
- Folate
- Potassium
- Beta-carotene, which converts in the body to vitamin A (especially high in red peppers)
- Numerous plant compounds including capsanthin, quercetin, and lutein
- Fiber

what can they do for me?

The plant compounds contained in peppers are powerful antioxidants known to have health benefits, such as preventing chronic conditions like heart disease and cancer. The high amounts of carotenoids in peppers may improve eye health, and they help to protect the retina against oxidative damage.

how to eat peppers

Peppers are another very versatile vegetable. Use them raw, on their own or with dips, or juice them. Stuff and bake them, or add them to a variety of other dishes such as pizzas and pasta. Roasted, stir-fried, charbroiled, canned; these are all delicious ways to prepare them.

varieties

Sweet bell peppers are commonly available in many varieties:

RED

ROMANO PEPPERS

YELLOW

ORANGE

other varieties

- **GREEN**: Green peppers are unripe versions of the red, orange, or yellow pepper

- **PURPLE**: Resembling a green or red bell pepper, this pepper is a stunning deep purple, which contrasts with its green flesh; it has a sweet flavor

- **WHITE**: This pepper is usually smaller than the green bell pepper; it has a crisp flavor and makes a good addition to salads

- **MINI SWEET PEPPER**: Similar to the usual bell pepper, this pepper is smaller and sweeter; it is good for roasting or frying

- **CUBANELLE PEPPER**: Also called Italian frying pepper or the banana pepper, this pepper is a long sweet pepper available in a variety of colors; it is has a thin skin so is suitable for roasting

how to cook peppers

type of veg	quantity for 2	quantity for 4	cooking vessel	quantity of liquid	salt	oil / butter

steam

type of veg	quantity for 2	quantity for 4	cooking vessel	quantity of liquid	salt	oil / butter
↑ Peppers ↓	2 red peppers		↑ steamer ↓	2 inches (5 cm) water in steamer	↑ ½ tablespoon ↓	1 tablespoon olive oil

bake/roast

type of veg	quantity for 2	quantity for 4	cooking vessel	quantity of liquid	salt	oil / butter
↑ Peppers ↓	↑ 2–3 red peppers ↓		↑ medium baking sheet ↓		↑ 1 teaspoon ↓	↑ 1 tablespoon olive oil ↓

fry

type of veg	quantity for 2	quantity for 4	cooking vessel	quantity of liquid	salt	oil / butter
↑ Peppers ↓	↑ 2–3 peppers (red, yellow, orange, or a combo) ↓		↑ large high-sided skillet ↓		↑ 1 teaspoon or to taste ↓	↑ 1 tablespoon olive oil ↓

soup

type of veg	quantity for 2	quantity for 4	cooking vessel	quantity of liquid	salt	oil / butter
↑ Peppers ↓		↑ 6 bell peppers, roasted, skins removed ↓	↑ large saucepan ↓	↑ 3⅓ cups (800 ml) vegetable broth ↓	↑ to taste ↓	↑ 3 tablespoons (45 ml) olive oil ↓

other ingredients	heat	with lid	cooking time	notes
1 tablespoon sherry vinegar, toasted sliced almonds, parsley	↑ medium ↓	↑ yes ↓	↑ 7–8 min. ↓	Steaming peppers results in quite a subtle flavor, which is pumped up when acid is added, such as sherry vinegar here. The crunch of sliced almonds adds some textural interest.
↑ 1 head garlic, cloves bashed, skins on ↓	↑ 400°F (200°C) ↓	↑ no ↓	↑ 40 min. ↓	Roasted red peppers like this make a wonderful addition to salads and rice bowls. The garlic should be sticky and sweet after cooking alongside the peppers, so make sure to incorporate them into your dish.
↑ 1 garlic clove, chopped; splash of balsamic or sherry vinegar ↓	↑ medium-high ↓	↑ no ↓	↑ 15 min. ↓	Fried or sautéed peppers make a great addition to any meal. Simply seed and slice the peppers into strips. Heat the oil in the pan, add the garlic, and cook for 1 minute before adding the peppers and salt. Cook, stirring occasionally until sweet and tender. Finish with a splash of acidity such as balsamic or sherry vinegar to enhance the sweetness. Pomegranate molasses would also work wonderfully here. Serve as is, or add herbs, nuts, or even some crumbled feta for a more substantial side.
↑ 4 garlic cloves, chopped; 1 red onion, diced; 5 sundried tomatoes; 1 lemon ↓	↑ medium ↓	↑ no ↓	↑ 10 min. ↓	Roasting the peppers first results in sweet and tender flesh and makes the skins a breeze to peel, allowing you to avoid any additional straining. However, if you aren't able to roast your peppers first, similarly great results can be achieved by simply sautéing the chopped peppers for a few minutes longer alongside the other aromatics before adding the broth. Purée the cooked soup to a smooth and silky consistency before gently reheating to serve.

PREP / COOK TIME

TIP

gluten-free / nut-free

15 min. / 40 min.

If the risotto is a little thick, then add a little hot water to loosen it before serving. For a dinner party treat, add grilled large prawns to the top.

Green pepper pesto risotto

Serves: 4–6

4½ cups (1.1 L) vegetable broth

½ cup (115 ml) extra virgin olive oil

2 onions, finely diced

5 garlic cloves, finely chopped

2 cups (400 g) arborio rice

2 cups (500 ml) white wine

½ cup (113 g) butter

salt and pepper

Pesto

2 green bell peppers

1¼ cups (150 g) toasted pistachios

1 garlic clove

juice of 1 lemon

½ cup (115 ml) extra virgin olive oil

5 cups (100 g) basil leaves, plus 1 handful to serve

1½ cups (150 g) finely grated Parmesan cheese, plus extra to serve

For the pesto, using tongs, place the peppers over an open flame on your stove, turning them as the skin starts to blacken. Keep turning until they are black all over. Let cool in a covered bowl.

Meanwhile, heat the broth gently in a pan over low heat.

Heat the olive oil in a large pan over medium heat, add the onions and garlic and fry for 10 minutes, or until soft. Add the rice and toast for 5 minutes. Pour in the wine and allow to reduce slightly. Add a ladleful of the hot broth and stir until it has evaporated, then continue this process until all the broth has been used. This should take 15–20 minutes. Reduce the heat to low while you make the pesto.

For the pesto, peel the charred skin off the peppers. Discard the seeds and tear the peppers into a blender. Add the nuts, garlic, lemon juice, olive oil, basil, and cheese and blend until smooth.

Stir the butter through the risotto and season to taste. Stir the pesto through the risotto and top with extra Parmesan and basil.

PREP / COOK TIME

15 min. / 40 min.

TIP   gluten-free

Roast extra peppers and keep covered in a bowl for
a few days in the fridge or jar covered in olive oil.

Charred red pepper salad

Serves: 4

8 red bell peppers, sliced
in half, seeded
1 head garlic, bashed
but skins intact
½ cup (115 ml) olive oil
⅔ cup (100 g) blanched
almonds
2 tablespoons white
wine vinegar
¾ cup (75 g) grated
Parmesan cheese
1 bunch of flat-leaf
parsley, leaves picked

Preheat the oven to 400°F (200°C).

Place the peppers in a roasting pan with the garlic and half
the olive oil and bake for 40 minutes, or until they have softened,
wrinkled, and charred a little.

Meanwhile, toast the almonds in a dry skillet, tossing until evenly
colored. Remove and add half the nuts to a blender with the
remaining olive oil, the vinegar, 2 halves of the peppers,
half the Parmesan, and half the parsley, and blend until smooth.

Spoon the pesto onto a platter and top with the remaining
peppers, garlic, and juices from the pan. Finish with the remaining
parsley leaves, nuts, and Parmesan.

One-pan baked couscous, pepper, & feta salad

Serves: 4

3 bell peppers, halved and seeded

½ cup (115 ml) olive oil

3 tablespoons rose harissa paste

1 head garlic, bashed

1¼ cups (200 g) couscous

grated zest and juice of 1 lemon

seeds of 1 pomegranate

7 oz. (200 g) feta, crumbled

1 handful of mint and parsley leaves

Preheat the oven to 350°F (180°C).

Roughly chop the peppers into bite-sized pieces and add to a snug-fitting baking dish. Drizzle over half the olive oil and toss in the harissa paste and garlic and mix very well. Roast for 15 minutes, or until sticky and a little soft.

Add the couscous and pour over ¾ cup (175 ml) boiling water and the lemon juice and zest. Cover with foil and place in the oven for 10–12 minutes. Remove and fluff the couscous up with a fork.

Sprinkle over the pomegranate seeds, feta, and herbs and serve.

Red pepper soup

Serves: 4

6 pointed or red bell peppers, seeded and roughly chopped

4 garlic cloves peeled and left whole

olive oil, for cooking

1 red onion, diced

5 sundried tomatoes

grated zest and juice of 1 lemon

3⅓ cups (800 ml) vegetable broth

1–2 tablespoons store-bought basil pesto

salt and pepper

grated Parmesan cheese, to serve

Preheat the oven to 400°F (200°C).

Place the red peppers and garlic cloves on a baking sheet. Drizzle with olive oil and season well with salt and pepper. Roast for 40 minutes, or until slightly charred.

Heat a little olive oil in a large heavy saucepan over medium heat, add the onion, and fry until soft and a little sticky. Add the cooked peppers to the pan and any juices together with the sundried tomatoes and lemon juice. Pour in the broth and bring to a boil. Reduce the heat and simmer for 10 minutes. Remove from the heat and, using a handheld blender, blend until smooth.

Ladle the soup into bowls and top with a little pesto, a drizzle of olive oil, and a sprinkling of lemon zest and grated Parmesan.

cauliflower

Cauliflower is another vegetable in the brassica family. The name derives from an Italian word meaning "cabbage family." Typically only the head is eaten. The head resembles that of broccoli but is composed of white flesh, sometimes called a "curd."

what's in it?

With only 5 g carbs in 100 g cauliflower, it is an excellent alternative to replace grains and legumes for a low-carb diet. 1 cup (100 g) chopped raw cauliflower contains:

- 27 calories
- 2 g protein
- 77% of daily vitamin C requirement
- 20% of daily vitamin K requirement
- Fiber

- Indole-3-carbinol (I3C), an antioxidant contained in many brassica family vegetables
- Sulforaphane
- Many minerals, such as calcium, magnesium, potassium, and phosphorus

what can it do for me?

Cauliflower's high fiber and water content (92%) make it a constipation preventive. Fiber increases the health of the digestive tract and is also thought to reduce inflammatory-related conditions, such as cardiovascular disease, diabetes, and cancer. The high content of the antioxidants sulforaphane and I3C has been found to help prevent cellular mutations and reduce the risk and further growth of some cancers.

how to eat cauliflower

Raw cauliflower is now being used much more in healthy dishes as a wheat alternative. Pulse the raw cauliflower in a blender to make cauliflower rice or use it to make a pizza dough. Otherwise cauliflower can be baked, steamed, and added to many dishes, such as curries and cheese bakes.

varieties

There are 4 major groups of cauliflower based on where in the world they are grown, but there are hundreds of varieties. They can also be grouped by color:

WHITE CLOUD

ORANGE BOUQUET

PURPLE HEAD

ROMANESCO

other varieties

Here are some less common varieties of cauliflower:

- **SNOWBALL**: An American heritage cauliflower, this variety has pure white snowball heads, which can be harvested quite small; this is a favorite to grow in gardens

- **SELF BLANCH**: This variety has bright white curds that are enclosed in leaves to protect it from the sun, hence the name

- **GRAFFITI**: This is a light magenta cauliflower, which turns purple when cooked

- **THE ORANGE BOUQUET**: Also called Cheddar cauliflower or Orange Burst, this relatively new variety owes its color to a genetic mutation

- **GREEN ROMANESCO**: This lime-green cauliflower has a crunchier texture and nuttier taste than ordinary cauliflowers

how to cook

type of veg	quantity for 2	cooking vessel	quantity of liquid	salt	oil / butter

steam

type of veg	quantity for 2	cooking vessel	quantity of liquid	salt	oil / butter
Cauliflower	½ large head cauliflower	steamer	2 inches (5 cm) water in steamer	½ tablespoon	1 tablespoon either

bake/roast

type of veg	quantity for 2	cooking vessel	quantity of liquid	salt	oil / butter
Cauliflower	½ large head cauliflower	medium baking sheet		1 teaspoon	1 tablespoon either

fry

type of veg	quantity for 2	cooking vessel	quantity of liquid	salt	oil / butter
Cauliflower	½ large head cauliflower	large nonstick skillet		½ teaspoon	2 tablespoons vegetable oil or ghee

soup

type of veg	quantity for 2	cooking vessel	quantity of liquid	salt	oil / butter
Cauliflower	8 cups (800 g) cauliflower florets	large saucepan	4 cups (1 L) broth, such as vegetable or chicken	to taste	1 tablespoon olive oil

rice

type of veg	quantity for 2	cooking vessel	quantity of liquid	salt	oil / butter
Cauliflower	1 large head cauliflower			to taste	

cauliflower

other ingredients	heat	with lid	cooking time	notes
2 tablespoons chopped herbs, such as parsley, chives, thyme, mint, etc.	↑ medium ↓	↑ yes ↓	↑ 6–7 min. ↓	Cut the cauliflower into large florets and discard the stem. Toss with butter, salt, pepper, and lots of chopped herbs.
	↑ 350°F (180°C) ↓	↑ no ↓	↑ 30 min. ↓	Simply roast cauliflower florets tossed in oil and salt for 30 minutes until golden and tender. If your cauliflower came with leaves, throw them in for the last 10 minutes of cooking for a delicious kale-like crisp.
1 teaspoon each ground spices, such as cumin, coriander, and turmeric; squeeze of lemon juice; chili flakes; parsley, chopped	↑ medium-high ↓	↑ no ↓	↑ 15 min. ↓	Separate cauliflower into small florets. Heat oil or ghee, add the cauliflower, and cook until almost cooked through and golden brown. Add any spices and salt and cook for 5 min. until cauliflower is tender. Add lemon juice, season to taste, and stir in chopped parsley.
1 onion, diced; 1 garlic clove, crushed; ground cumin; ground coriander; ⅔ cup (150 ml) heavy cream	↑ medium ↓	↑ no ↓	↑ 20–30 min. ↓	Heat the oil in the pan, add the onion and fry until softened. Add the garlic and cook for 1 min. Add the spices and chopped cauliflower and cook, stirring, for several min. Add the broth and simmer for 8–10 min. Cool slightly, then blend. Add cream and warm through.
while not strictly needed, consider adding complementary flavors such as chopped soft herbs, ground spices, or lemon zest				Pulse the cauliflower in a food processor until it is a coarse rice-like consistency. It can be used as is, warmed through in a pan for 1–2 min. with a splash of oil or piece of butter, or added to more substantial dishes, such as stir-fries or curries.

For a vegan version, use vegetable broth instead of the chicken broth, olive oil instead of the butter, and leave out the Parmesan.

Cauli steaks with polenta mash & crispy sage

Serves: 4

1 large cauliflower or 2 small

1 cup (240 ml) extra virgin olive oil

grated zest and juice of 1 lemon

5 garlic cloves, peeled and bashed

¾ cup (100 g) drained capers

3⅓ cups (800 ml) whole milk

1 chicken bouillon cube dissolved in 2 cups (500 ml) freshly boiled water

1½ cups (250 g) instant polenta

1½ cups (150 g) grated Parmesan cheese, plus extra to serve

1 bunch of sage

salt and pepper

Preheat the oven to 425°F (220°C).

Slice 1¼-inch (3 cm) thick rounds of the cauliflower so you have 4 equal size steaks. Place on a large baking sheet and drizzle over ½ cup (120 ml) of the olive oil, the lemon juice and zest, garlic, and capers, and season really well with salt and pepper. Place in the oven for 20 minutes, then turn the cauliflower gently and cook for another 20 minutes.

Fifteen minutes before the cauliflower is ready, make the polenta. Bring the milk and broth to a boil in a large pan. Pour the polenta into the pan in a steady stream, then stir vigorously for 10–12 minutes until the mixture is smooth and thick. Add the grated cheese and 3½ tablespoons (50 ml) of the olive oil and season generously.

Heat the remaining 4½ tablespoons (65 ml) olive oil in a large skillet over medium heat. Add the sage and fry for 3 minutes, or until crisp. Remove and set aside. Season with a little salt.

Spoon the polenta onto plates and top with the cauliflower steaks and the extra crispy bits in the pan. Sprinkle over the sage leaves and a little extra Parmesan.

10 min. / 30 min.

Serve as a feast with the sweet potato fries on page 94 and 40 clove roast garlic chicken on page 176.

Cauli crispy buffalo wings

Serves: 4 as a snack or side

1 large cauliflower, leaves discarded, and cut into large florets

1 teaspoon sweet paprika

1 teaspoon garlic powder

5 tablespoons rice flour

¾ cup (100 g) self-rising flour

1 cup (230 ml) sparkling water

⅔ cup (150 ml) buffalo hot sauce

½ cup (113 g) butter

2 celery stems, finely sliced and leaves reserved

salt and pepper

Preheat the oven to 400°F (200°C). Line a large baking sheet with parchment paper and set aside.

Place the cauliflower in a large bowl with the paprika and garlic powder and toss very well. Season generously with salt and pepper.

Mix the flours and sparkling water together in another bowl until it is a thick pancake-like batter. Pour the batter over the cauliflower and toss well until the cauliflower is coated.

Tip the mixture onto the prepared baking sheet, making sure the cauliflower isn't too close together, and bake for 30 minutes, tossing occasionally, until it is golden and crisp.

Meanwhile, pour the hot sauce into a small saucepan and place over high heat. Once bubbling, add the butter and simmer for a few minutes, whisking constantly, until thickened and glossy. Remove from the heat and set aside.

Once the cauliflower is ready, pour over the sauce and sprinkle over the celery and celery leaves.

PREP / COOK TIME

10 min. / 10 min.

TIP

vegetarian / gluten-free / nut-free

Process extra cauliflower and keep in an airtight container in the fridge for up to a week to make a speedy rice supper whenever needed.

Stir-fried cauliflower rice

Serves: 2

1 head cauliflower, large outer leaves removed

1 bunch of cilantro, leaves picked and stems chopped

5 garlic cloves, peeled

2½-inch (6 cm) piece of ginger, peeled and grated

2 green chili peppers, seeded and roughly chopped

4 tablespoons ghee

7 oz. (200 g) green beans, sliced in half

2 large eggs

1 lime, cut into wedges

mint leaves, to garnish

Roughly chop the cauliflower, discarding the larger inner stem. Place in a food processor and pulse until it is a coarse rice-like consistency. Scoop out and set aside.

Add the cilantro leaves and stems to the food processor along with the garlic, ginger, chili peppers, and half the ghee, and blend until it is a smooth bright green paste.

Add 1 tablespoon of the remaining ghee to a large skillet and place over high heat. Tip in the cauliflower rice and keep moving it around the pan for 5 minutes, or until lightly colored. Tip in the green paste and green beans and stir-fry for another 3 minutes.

Add the remaining ghee to a large nonstick skillet and place over high heat. Once hot, fry the eggs until the yolk is runny and the whites are crispy.

Scoop the rice onto plates and top with the crispy egg and a lime wedge. Garnish with mint and serve.

PREP / COOK TIME

TIP

vegetarian / gluten-free / nut-free

30 min. / 1 hr. 30 min.

Serve with some turmeric-and-ginger-roasted new potatoes, raita, and flatbreads for a feast night.

Whole roasted tandoori cauli with baked lemon & herbs

Serves: 4

1⅔ cups (400 g) plain yogurt
2 white onions, peeled
1 head garlic, peeled and roughly chopped
2½-inch (6 cm) piece of ginger, peeled and roughly chopped
2 green chili peppers, chopped
3 tablespoons tandoori curry paste
1 lemon
1 large cauliflower, with leaves if possible
1 large handful of cilantro and mint
salt

Preheat the oven to 375°F (190°C).

Place the yogurt, onions, garlic, ginger, chili peppers, tandoori paste, lemon juice, and 1 teaspoon of salt in a food processor and purée until smooth. Chop the flesh of the lemon into small chunks and stir through the sauce.

Slice a deep cross in the bottom of the cauliflower stem and discard any discolored leaves on the cauliflower.

Place the cauliflower in a heavy saucepan that fits the cauliflower snugly. Pour over the paste and massage it in. If you have time, leave to marinate overnight.

Cover with a lid and bake for 1 hour. Increase the oven temperature to 500°F (250°C), uncover, and bake for 20 minutes to char.

Spoon all the marinade in the bottom of the pan over the cauliflower and sprinkle over the herbs before serving.

15 min. / 1 hr. 10 min.

Best-ever cauliflower & cheese

Serves: 4–6

½ cup (113 g) unsalted butter, plus ¼ cup (57 g) for the topping

6 garlic cloves, sliced

¾ cup (100 g) all-purpose flour

3⅓ cups (800 ml) whole milk

5 oz. (150 g) mature Cheddar cheese

2¼ lb. (1 kg) cauliflower, cut into large florets

5 oz. (150 g) stale sourdough bread

½ bunch of thyme, leaves picked

½ cup (60 g) hazelnuts

salt and pepper

Preheat the oven to 350°F (180°C).

Heat the ½ cup (113 g) butter in a pan over medium heat, add the garlic slices and fry for 2 minutes, or until golden. Scoop out the garlic and set aside.

Stir the flour into the garlic butter and mix for a minute to make a paste, then gradually add the milk, whisking, until smooth. Grate in half the Cheddar and season with salt and pepper to taste. Remove from the heat.

Arrange the cauliflower florets in the base of an 8 × 12-inch (20 × 30 cm) high-sided baking dish and pour over the cheese sauce.

Place the bread in a food processor and pulse into breadcrumbs, then pulse in the thyme leaves, hazelnuts, the reserved crispy garlic, and the ¼ cup (55 g) butter. Season well. Sprinkle the breadcrumb mix evenly over the cauliflower cheese and bake for 1 hour, or until golden and cooked through.

Index

acknowledgments

Every time I sit down to start a book, I think about the huge team behind me helping me make it happen. It would be nothing without the large help of all the people involved.

First, I'd like to thank Catie Ziller for continuing to believe in my abilities to write and style a book. Thank you for always being so on the ball and guiding me through every step. I look forward to collaborating with you for years to come.

Issy Croker, you will forever be my work wife and incredibly talented friend. I owe you for the long days and continually forcing you to try everything I cook because your opinion means so much to me. You make the images look so beautiful and do it with complete ease.

Thank you for constantly being by my side. Thank you, Saskia, Kitty, Amber, and Daniella for being my incredible food assistants across the many shoot days—you were all brilliant.

Thank you Narroway Studio for letting us use your beautiful studio once again for nearly 3 weeks straight. It the most calming studio on hectic days to be in.

Kathy Steer, thank you for being such a strong and dedicated editor. I know the recipes will be foolproof and we totally have you to thank for this. Your easy and friendly attitude to it all is totally reassuring and I feel totally supported by you.

Michelle, thank you for all your work on the design. Good design is so important and can carry a book, and you do it all in a flash of ease.

Rushton, my incredible fruit and vegetable supplier who I'm sure grew sick of my many calls trying to track down different varieties of fruit and veg and went above and beyond to help me. I won't miss driving to see you at 4am, but thank you.

Hardie Grant
NORTH AMERICA

Hardie Grant North America

2912 Telegraph Ave
Berkeley, CA 94705

hardiegrantusa.com

ISBN 9781958417515

ISBN: 9781958417522
(eBook)

Printed in China

Library of congress cataloging-in-publication data is available upon request.

Copyright text © 2019 by Marabout

For the Marabout edition:

Publisher: Catie Ziller
Author: Emily Ezekiel
Photographer: Issy Croker
Photography Assistants:
Saskia Sidey & Kitty Coles
Designer: Michelle Tilly
Project Editor: Kathy Steer